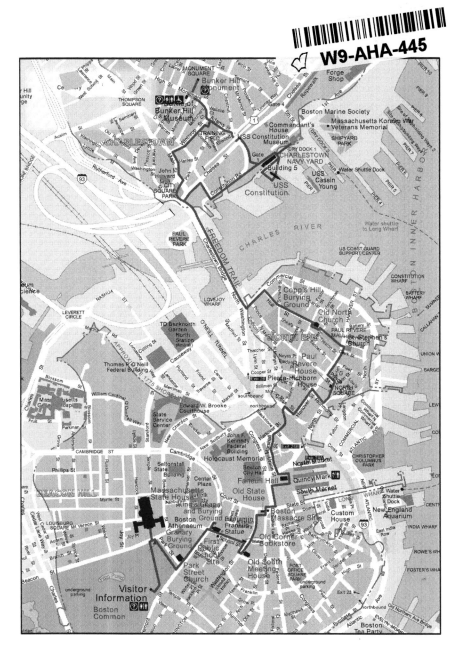

Freedom Trail Map w/outline of Boston in 1775

**Old North Church seen from Copp's Hill Burying Ground –
looking at the steeple where the "two if by sea" lanterns would
be seen by Patriots in Charlestown before Paul Revere's Ride**

View of Boston's North End skyline with Old North Church & the Custom House seen from site of the USS Constitution

Long Wharf & the Custom House seen from the Charlestown Water Shuttle approaching Boston

Interior of Old North Church, oldest church in Boston

Old City Hall by the site of America's first public school

Freedom Trail Boston

Ultimate Tour & History Guide
Tips, Secrets & Tricks

Steve Gladstone

http://www.stevestravelguide.com

steve@stevestravelguide.com

Copyright & Disclaimer

Freedom Trail Boston - Ultimate Tour & History Guide - Tips, Secrets & Tricks

Copyright © 2012, 2013, 2014 Steve Gladstone. All rights reserved.

No part of this publication may be copied, stored in a retrieval system, or transmitted in any form by any means, electronic, mechanical, recording or otherwise, except brief extracts for the purpose of review, and no part of this publication may be sold or hired, without the written permission of the author except as permitted under Sections 107 or 108 of the 1976 United States Copyright Act, or through payment of the appropriate per-copy fee. Thank you for respecting the hard work of this author.

Be advised although the author has taken all reasonable care in preparing this book, we make no warranty about the accuracy or completeness of its content and to the maximum extent permitted, disclaim all liability from its use including, but not limited to, any inconvenience, loss or injury sustained by any person relying on information or advice contained in this book.

ISBN-10: 1479132144
ISBN-13: 978-1479132140

The Freedom Trail® is a registered trademark of The Freedom Trail Foundation, Inc. This book is independently published and not affiliated with the Freedom Trail Foundation.

Old North Church® is a registered trademark of Christ Church in the City of Boston, Inc.

Table of Contents

Introduction

Welcome

Web translate and narration link:
(http://www.stevestravelguide.com/?p=1404)

Congratulations on your Boston visit - whether for an afternoon, a day or two, a week, or more. It's a great city.

Boston has everything you want - world class museums, fantastic restaurants, shopping, sports, music, theater and history. It's a unique and charming place that can feed almost any passion. And, there are great options for any budget.

If you are interested in its history, especially the Freedom Trail and Colonial Boston, this Guide will help you make the most of your visit. It is full of insider tips, secrets and tricks not known by even the most ardent of professional guides.

You will find everything you need to know about the official Freedom Trail Stops (there are 16 of them), interesting "unofficial" Stops, (I cover over 50 of them), and even the most interesting and historic restaurants. Maps, including web access to an interactive, zoomable, photo-packed Google Map (a complete tour-guide by itself) are included. To make the most of your visit, there are itineraries for one-half, one or two day tours.

In addition, I've included tips for the most worthwhile side trips to Harvard Square, Lexington & Concord, Adams NHP and the Harbor Islands.

There is even a Budget Tips section - Boston is a big city, with big-city prices. There are many tips to moderate your visit's cost without compromising the fun - and even include a lobster.

More than just a description of the Freedom Trail Stops, there is also the background history and information to help you appreciate what you visit.

All the information is provided at cascading levels of detail - from simple overviews to detailed descriptions of every Stop and events that include the Boston Tea Party, Paul Revere's Ride, the Battles of Lexington and Concord, and the Battle of Bunker Hill.

Choose just what you want to know, you can always return for more. Finally, there are recommendations for the best internet links and books, much of it free.

The influence Boston had on the thinking and actions that led to the American Revolution was extraordinary. Without Boston and its unique history, the American colonies break with Great Britain may have still happened, but not when and how it did. The Guide brings this to life and helps you to appreciate Boston's really amazing impact.

Even though I've been a Bostonian since 1970 and have always been interested in history, there were three "ahas" that developed as I wrote this Guide. These helped me appreciate The Freedom Trail much more. They may be of interest, and they just might help your visit be more fun.

1. **First, Puritan philosophy is at the root of the thinking that led to the American Revolution**. Everyone knows that the Puritans who founded Boston left England seeking religious freedom, but they also brought with them their own brand of powerful ideas. Around those ideas they molded a unique religious, democratic, and fiercely independent society that hated outsiders (like the British) telling them what to do. These ideas shaped the leaders that shaped the Revolution - including Ben Franklin, Samuel Adams, John Adams, John Hancock, and Paul Revere.

2. **Second, Boston's Puritans were able to establish and run their own society only because England neglected them for three generations**. By the time England tried to reassert control, it was too late, and they bungled the efforts they did make. The tension, disputes, and outright fighting between the Puritan New Englanders and the Anglican English is the essence of most of the Freedom Trail sites.

3. **Third, Boston's Colonial-era topography played a critical role in historical events**. What you visit today is over 50% landfill and many of its hills have been leveled. Places you will walk, such as the area around Faneuil Hall, were actually part of the harbor when Boston was founded. Boston was practically an island - dependent on the harbor for its economy and supplies. When the port of Boston

was closed after the Tea Party in 1774, until the Siege was lifted in 1776, the city was completely isolated. Understanding this will provide extra meaning.

The Freedom Trail

The original idea for the Freedom Trail was conceived by William Schofield, a long-time journalist for the now defunct Boston newspaper, the Herald Traveler. In 1951, Schofield had the idea for a walking path that connected Boston's great collection of local landmarks. With the support of local historians, politicians and businessmen, the Freedom Trail was born.

The Freedom Trail is a 2.7 mile red brick path (mostly brick - some lines are painted) that connects 16 significant historic sites, referred to as "Stops" throughout the Guide. It starts at Boston Common and officially ends at the Bunker Hill Monument in Charlestown. Most of the Stops are free and many are handicapped accessible, but some may be difficult to navigate for non-walkers. For the few that charge admission, there are discounted tickets available (see the Budget Tips chapter).

In addition to the official Stops, there are many other interesting things to see and experience near the Trail. These unofficial Stops are often directly related to the Freedom Trail and Colonial Boston, but some are simply interesting places. I've made every effort to cover everything relevant in the Guide - if you think I've missed something important, please email me and I'll include note it in an update to the custom Google Map and app that complement the Guide.

Enjoy, Boston is a great city and The Freedom Trail is a national treasure.

How to Use the Guide

This Guide is available in print or eBook formats. To read this on a Kindle, iPad, other eReader/tablet or Smartphone, it is recommended that you download a version for those devices from Amazon.com or other retailer.

When reading as an eBook, there are many hyperlinks that facilitate moving quickly between your areas of interest. When "live," i.e. connected to the internet, you also have access to additional detailed information, including zoomable Google maps, video, and other items to enhance your visit.

To maintain as many of the features of an eBook in this paper version, I have embedded selected Quick Response Codes (QR Codes) throughout the Guide. Scanning these codes from a Smartphone will take you directly to the associated web sites, which have live, clickable links. There are also textual link listings if you do not have access to a QR scanner.

When using the Guide as a personal tour guide when visiting the Freedom Trail, almost everything you need is provided within the section about any specific Stop. Essential information, including a high-level Stop description, operating hours, costs, phone numbers, web sites, and public transport information is in each Stop's "Overview" section. More detailed Stop information is in each Stop's "Background Information" section.

The most significant background historical information is found in the Time Line, Boston History and North End chapters. If you are reading the Guide for historical context, you should start with those sections.

Budget Tips and the Historic Restaurant Guide are provided at the end of the book along with sections on Sources and recommended Related Information.

Web references are either embedded within the text or, as part of the Additional Links & References chapter at the end of the book.

Maps, Getting Around, & Free Touring Apps

In the front of the Guide is an extract from one of the most illustrative maps available for the Freedom Trail, the "Park Map with Outline of 1775 Boston Shoreline" from the National Park Service. It is strongly recommended you download and print this along with the other excellent free maps from the National Park Service website. References for this and other NPS maps can be found in the Additional Links and References chapter at the end of the book.

If you have web access, the best map is a custom Google Map, created especially for the Guide, available on the web at http://goo.gl/maps/LhFI. It is fully zoomable, interactive, has detailed touring information, links and photos about each of the official and unofficial Freedom Trail Stops, restaurants and other attractions. The Google Map is a living map - it is being enhanced as I learn more and get tips from readers. It is the perfect companion to this Guide.

Better still is the free companion free Android or iPhone app available from Google Play or iTunes. The app performs far better than using the map, has many additional features and offers many more points of interest in Boston and surrounding towns. A must if you have a smartphone.

Here are the respective QR codes for both the Google Map and the App on Google Play and iTunes:

If you prefer to pick up paper maps once you reach Boston, they are available at either of the National Park Service Visitor Centers. There is a brand new Visitor Center on the first floor of Faneuil Hall (Stop 11) and one in the Charlestown Navy Yard, right next to the USS Constitution.

Maps and other tour information can also be obtained at The Freedom Trail Visitor Center on Boston Common (Stop 1). Boston is a walking city, and it is strongly recommended that you walk or take public transportation. Boston has the MBTA, the oldest subway system in the United States (called the "T" by locals). There are T stops close to most of the Freedom Trail Stops, although the Charlestown and North End Stops require moderate walks from the closest station. There are public transportation references in the Overview section of each Freedom Trail Stop. You can also see public transportation references when using the Google Map and app.

Auto-Translate the Guide to Foreign Languages

For readers who prefer to read the Guide in a different native language, including Spanish, French, German, Italian, Japanese, Mandarin and others, I've implemented a web-based auto-translate feature. Go to the "auto-translate" link (embedded in the Guide's text) by typing the URL into a browser or by scanning the associated QR code. Once on the web page, click the desired language flag to select and view the translated text.

Tall Ships at the Charlestown Navy Yard

All translations are performed by a standard translation engine, so it may take a second or two to process. And, the translation may not be perfect. But if you don't read English well, this can help you enjoy more of your Freedom Trail visit.

Auto-translate is available for the Introduction and Touring & Itineraries, Boston Background & History, North End and Budget Tips chapters as well as for each official Stop.

The first time you access auto-translate links for the Boston Background & History chapter you will need to enter a password. The password is the first word of the third paragraph in that chapter (the paragraph before the 1645 map extract) - be sure to capitalize the word correctly. When using the auto-translate version, this chapter is broken into five parts reading.

Audio Narration

To enhance your visit, streaming audio narration for virtually all of the historical Stops is available via the internet using the same QR codes that are used for auto-translate. The narration is similar, but not identical to the text; additional information may be provided. Once on the web page, you will see a simple audio player that you can use to play, pause and move around the narration.

Updates and Supplemental Information

Additional and supplemental information, new maps, updates and corrections are available at:
http://www.stevestravelguide.com/?p=1737

Touring & Suggested Itineraries

Self-Guided or a Tour?

So, should you take a guided tour or guide yourself? This book and the associated narrations contain most of what a paid guide will share (actually more), and allows you to go at your own pace. However, a group tour can be a lot of fun and may engage you in a way that a self-guided tour will not.

There are excellent free tours given by National Park Service (NPS) rangers. Most of the paid guided tours cost $12-15 per adult (some have senior discounts) and $8-10 for children.

Most tours run an hour or an hour and a half and concentrate on selected parts of the Freedom Trail - such as the downtown portions (Boston Common to Faneuil Hall - Stops 1 - 11), the North End (Paul Revere House, Old North Church & Copp's Hill - Stops 12 - 14), or Charlestown (USS Constitution and Bunker Hill - Stops 15 - 16).

Within these time constraints, the guided tours do not allow you to spend much time within any of the Stops and will often not enter the Stops at all. Almost all will skip entering those Stops that charge a special admission fee (Old South Meeting House, Old State House and the Paul Revere House). Check for times/availability from November through March.

Recommended tour companies include:

National Park Service. The National Park Service (NPS) provides free ranger-guided tours and lectures including two 60 minute tours of the Freedom Trail (one covering downtown, the other the North End - combine them for a more complete visit), the USS Cassin Young, USS Constitution, and Faneuil Hall. They are highly recommended, well done, and the price is right. Some tours are attendance limited and first come, first served, so get there in time to get an admission sticker, usually 1/2 hour before the scheduled start. Call (617) 242 5642 for information.

The Freedom Trail Foundation. The Freedom Trail Foundation is the official voice of the Freedom Trail, and some of the proceeds from their tours goes to support the Trail. They offer a variety of quality tours given by costumed actors.

Boston By Foot. Boston By Foot is a non-profit organization that uses unpaid volunteer guides that are well trained and have in-depth knowledge. They offer a variety of tours, including some geared to children. You do not need an advance ticket, just show up and pay the guide. Their approach is more in depth than many other companies, and they are very good

There are many other quality tour companies, some with specialty tours such as for photographers or historic pub crawls. Search Google for "Boston Walking Tours" or TripAdvisor for "Freedom Trail, Boston."

Suggested Itineraries

The entire Freedom Trail is only 2.7 miles, but seeing it all in one day will be difficult, especially if you want to spend time visiting any Stop. To help you plan, I've provided a quick assessment of each of the official 16 Stops, its significance to the Revolutionary period, and the recommended time needed for a visit.

Beneath the Stop Review section below, you will find itinerary recommendations with alternatives for 1/2 day and full day self-guided visits. For a two day visit, combine two of the day or four of the 1/2 day itineraries. Most of the downtown Stops (1 through 11) are close together. If including a guided tour, plan accordingly based on what that tour covers.

Walking directly from Boston Common to Faneuil Hall is only about .6 miles (1 km) and takes less than 15 minutes. Walking from downtown Stop 11 (Faneuil Hall) to Stop 12 (Paul Revere House) in the North End takes 10-15 minutes. The Charlestown Stops are another 15+ minute walk from the last Stop in the North End (Copp's Hill Burying Ground), and there is a 10+ minute walk between the USS Constitution and Bunker Hill.

Stop Review:

Stop 1 - Boston Common. A great old park, but unless you want to walk around and enjoy the outdoors, there is not much of prime historical importance. There is a good playground for younger children at Frog Pond.

Stop 2 - The State House. There are excellent guided tours and it is a fascinating and elegant old building, Plan 1.5-2 hours to pass through security and take the tour. While it is worthwhile, there is not much relating to the Revolutionary period as the State House was built after the Revolution. Take the time to view St. Gauden's Robert Gould Shaw & MA 54th Memorial across the street at the edge of Boston Common.

Stop 3 - Park Street Church. Closed for viewing except during the summer. Unless you take a tour, it will not take much time. There is little of primary Revolutionary significance.

Stop 4 - Granary Burying Ground. This is the final resting spot for Samuel Adams, John Hancock, Paul Revere, the Boston Massacre victims, Mother Goose and others. Plan about 15 minutes to walk through.

Stop 5 - King's Chapel. Great old church usually open for viewing. Plan 15 minutes to walk through, more to take the Bell & Bones tour.

Stop 5a - King's Chapel Burying Ground. The oldest in Boston, plan about 10 minutes to walk through and view the old stones. Not much of Revolutionary significance as the Burying Ground was full well before 1700.

Stop 6 - Boston Latin, Old City Hall, Franklin Statue. Everything is outside (there is no interior viewing of Old City Hall). Plan 5-10 minutes to view the outside plaques. If you want to see the Province House steps, plan for another 5 minutes to walk up Province Street.

Stop 7 - Old Corner Book Store. You will walk by and see the house, which now houses a Chipotle Mexican Grill. Nothing to tour.

Stop 8 - Old South Meeting House. Plan 1/2+ hour to view inside and the exhibits. The Meeting House is interesting given the number of important Revolutionary-era meetings that took place here. There are interpretive exhibits that place the building and its events in history and a good three dimensional map of Revolutionary-era Boston that highlights key locations - fascinating given the city's changing topography. Check their web site for other programs. Benjamin Franklin's birthplace and the Irish Memorial are directly across the street and are quick to see.

Stop 9 - Old State House. The Old State House features excellent docent-given tours and talks that cover the building and Revolutionary events. The museum has some good displays and exhibits. Plan about an hour or more to visit and take a tour. Highly worthwhile.

Stop 10- Boston Massacre Site. This is a plaque embedded in the street directly below the balcony of the Old State House. This is a walk-by with a photo opportunity.

Stop 11 - Faneuil Hall. This is a great old and important building. Go inside and enjoy a ranger-led talk (given every 30 minutes). Plan for 30-45 minutes to visit the Hall. The Faneuil Hall Marketplace (Quincy Market) is located next door, and is a good place to stop, get something to eat or shop. Plan accordingly. The new National Park Service Visitor Center is located on the first floor of Faneuil Hall.

Note: From Faneuil Hall, it is a 15 minute walk to the next official Stop, the Paul Revere House, in the North End. On the way, you pass some interesting unofficial Stops in the Blackstone Block - the Holocaust Memorial, Union Oyster House, Marshall Street, and the Ebenezer Hancock House. The Blackstone Block is also a good, less commercial place to break or eat. Some of the local restaurants feature good lobster specials at lunch.

Stop 12 - Paul Revere House. Built in 1680, it is the oldest structure remaining in Boston. It is a good example of a period dwelling and you will gain insights into Paul Revere's life. The costumed docents provide interesting descriptions of the house and the Revere family. Visiting is worthwhile, but the house is small, consisting of only four rooms. Plan for about 1/2 hour.

Note: It is about a 10 minute walk through the North End to the next stop. The North End is also an excellent place to stop for lunch. It has a very European feel and many wonderful restaurants.

Stop 13 - Old North Church. A beautiful and important church, the oldest remaining in Boston. A walk through takes 15 minutes, the Behind-the-Scenes tour another 30. A must visit.

Stop 14 - Copp's Hill Burying Ground. A 5 minute walk up hill from the Old North Church. Plan about 10-15 minutes to walk through the Burying Ground. There are a few interesting graves, a headstone used by the British for target practice, and a nice view of the harbor.

Note: From here there is another 15+ minute walk across the bridge to Charlestown and the next Stop, the USS Constitution.

Stop 15 - USS Constitution and the Charlestown Navy Yard. Visiting the Constitution and the Museum can easily be a half day visit. For the Constitution alone, plan at least an hour to pass through security, view the small museum and take the guided tour of the ship. The very good USS Constitution Museum (different from the small museum attached to the Constitution), is worth another hour. A walk around the WWII Destroyer USS Cassin Young will take another 1/2 hour. Walking around the Navy Yard area is also a pleasure; there is only one few restaurants in the Yard. This is a highly worthwhile 1/2 day, especially for children, who will enjoy exploring the ships.

Note: There is another 15 minute walk between the Charlestown Navy Yard and the Bunker Hill Monument and Museum. For a historic lunch, try the Warren Tavern, which is only a short detour between the two sites.

Stop 16 - Bunker Hill Monument. To tour the monument area, plan about 15-20 minutes, unless you plan to make the 294-step ascent to the top. That is a fun activity and provides a spectacular view of Boston and the surrounding area. If climbing the Monument, plan 1/2 hour. To visit the Bunker Hill Museum, which is excellent and best seen before the monument, plan another 1/2 to full hour. The museum features exhibits on the battle and Charlestown history, and has Ranger-guided programs - great for children. If you have time, visit the Museum before the Monument. Highly recommended.

1/2 Day Tour Alternatives

Option 1: (Downtown) Walk by Stops 1 - 3, visit Stops 3 - 5, walk by 6-8, visit 9, walk by 10, and visit 11. Lunch and break at Faneuil Hall Market or the Blackstone Block area.

Option 2: (Downtown and North End): Walk by Stops 1 - 3, visit Stops 3 - 5, walk by 6- 10, visit 11, walk by 12, visit 13 and 14. Lunch and break in Faneuil Hall Market, the Blackstone Block or the North End.

Option 3: (Charlestown - USS Constitution and Bunker Hill): Visit Stop 15 USS Constitution (bypass the Constitution Museum and USS Cassin Young), visit Bunker Hill Monument and Museum. Lunch at the Warren Tavern or at the Navy Yard.

Option 4: (Charlestown, USS Constitution): Spend a full 1/2 day visiting the USS Constitution, the Museum, USS Cassin Young and walk around the Navy Yard. Lunch at the Navy Yard or across the Bridge in the North End.

Option 5: (A little Downtown, free ranger-guided tour, North End, USS Constitution - requires a lot of walking and time coordination): Start at Stop 11, Faneuil Hall, listen to the Great Hall talk and take the NPS North End tour, visit Stops 13 - 15, then take the Water Shuttle back to Long Wharf.

Full Day Tour Alternatives

Boston and the North End: Walk by Stops 1-3, visit Stops 3-5, walk by 6-7, visit 8 - 9, walk by 10, visit 11, lunch or break in Faneuil Hall Market, the Blackstone Block or the North End, visit 12-14.

Charlestown: spend a full 1/2 day visiting the USS Constitution, the Constitution Museum, USS Cassin Young and walk around the Navy Yard, lunch around the Navy Yard or at the Warren Tavern, visit the Bunker Hill Monument and Museum.

If you want to visit the entire Freedom Trail in a single day, it is recommended that you combine Options 2 and 3. It will be busy and there is a lot of walking, but you will have a great time.

What Would I Do?

Without question, if I only had a half-day, I'd recommend Option 5, especially with kids. This requires planning to fit in the National Park Service ranger tours, but is absolutely worth it. Start at Faneuil Hall and attend a Great Hall ranger talk (every 1/2 hour) and get a sticker for the ranger-tour that goes to the North End (currently at 12, 2 & 3 PM - stickers available 1/2 hour prior. Confirm times at the NPS visitor center.) After the ranger tour, visit Old North Church (Stop 13), walk through Stop 14, then walk quickly to Stop 15 and take the USS Constitution tour. Take the Water Shuttle back to Long Wharf (every 1/2 hour during non-commuting hours). Grab lunch where you can.

If I only had half a day, wanted to self-guide, and could not coordinate times for Option 5, I'd recommend Option 2 with a lobster lunch in the Blackstone Block. See as much as you can, and the North End has fantastic character and feel. Don't miss a Faneuil Hall tour or a visit to the Old State House. If you are not from New England, the lobster is not to be missed.

If I had a full day, combine Options 2 and 3. The downtown stops are great and I love the Navy Yard and USS Constitution (it is easy to spend too much time here). Bunker Hill and the Bunker Hill museum are excellent. Have a lobster lunch in the Blackstone Block or grab some character and a Paul Revere Burger at the Warren Tavern in Charlestown (I'd choose the lobster, but it may be early in your day).

Mariners' House in North Square

Ceiling in the Custom House (1849), just off the Freedom Trail

Stop 1 – Boston Common

Oldest Public Park in the US

Purchased in 1634 from William Blaxton (Blackstone), the reclusive hermit and first white settler of the Shawmut peninsula.

Free

The Common is a public park

Official website:

http://www.cityofboston.gov/freedomtrail/bostoncommon.asp

617-536-4100

Handicap access: the park is generally accessible, but there are some steps at the exit to Beacon Street, which is required to access the State House, Freedom Trail Stop 2.

Restrooms are located in the Visitor Center, by Tremont Street

Public Transportation - Red or Green lines to the Park Street Station

Web translate and narration link:
(http://www.stevestravelguide.com/?p=1231)

Background Information

The Boston Common is the oldest public park in the United States. It was originally the pasture of William Blaxton (Blackstone). Blaxton was a reclusive hermit and the first white resident of the Shawmut (its Native American / Algonquian name) peninsula. Blaxton subsequently sold the Common property to the Puritans in 1634 for £30.

In 1630, the Puritans landed in Salem, about 40 miles to the north. They migrated south to Charlestown, and were in desperate need of a better water supply. Boston had an abundant fresh spring, and Blaxton invited the Puritans to move to the peninsula to share it.

As it was "common" land, the Common's 44 acres have been used for many purposes. For most of its early life it was the site of stocks for punishing criminals as well as public executions. The gallows remained in the park until 1817. For most of its history it was open grazing land, although cows were official evicted in 1830. It was also used as a town dump, but that activity was outlawed in 1652.

During the period of the British occupation of Boston, troops were quartered on the Common. On April 18, 1775, the troops departed from the Common's northwest corner for their raid on Lexington and Concord and the "shot heard round the world." At the time, the Common bordered the Charles River; the land to the west of the Common has since been filled-in.

Over the years the Common has been the site of many gatherings, concerts and celebrations. Notable events include visits by Martin Luther King in 1965 and Pope John Paul II in 1979. The Common was declared a U.S. National Historic Landmark in 1987.

Boston Common is a great place to wander, especially on a nice day and with children. If your children are young, try the Frog Pond area, which features a playground and snack bar. There is a good parking lot underneath the Common - enter on Charles Street.

Below find a listing of some of the Common's highlights.

The Visitor Center - Freedom Trail Start

The Freedom Trail officially starts from the Visitor Center, which is very close to the entrance to the Park Street MBTA station. The Visitor Center has Freedom Trail information or you can purchase guided tours given by actor-guides dressed in colonial garb. Alternatively, just take off by yourself by using this Guide and following the red path from in front of the Visitor Center to the next stop, the Massachusetts State House.

Parkman Bandstand

The Parkman Bandstand was built in 1912 in honor of George Parkman, who had willed $5 million to the parks of Boston. Its site was originally Cow (or Horse) Pond – which was filled in after cattle grazing was prohibited in 1830.

Soldiers and Sailors Monument

The Soldiers and Sailors Monument is on top of Flagstaff Hill, the tallest hill in the Common. Completed in 1877, it honors troops that perished in the Civil War.

The monument is 126 feet high and carved from white granite. There are four bas-relief tablets at the base of the column. The column is topped by a female figure titled America. She wears a crown of thirteen stars and holds the United States flag, a sword, and a laurel wreath in her hands.

Central Burying Ground

Dating from 1756, the Central Burying Ground is one of the oldest burial grounds in Boston. It is the last resting place of Gilbert Stuart (the artist who painted the portrait of George Washington used as the model for the one dollar bill) and many who died during the Battle of Bunker Hill. Enter the Burying Ground from Tremont Street.

Frog Pond

Frog Pond is a great place for skating in the winter and wading or playing in the summer. Starting at the end of June, there is a spray pool that provides a cooling diversion for those 12 and under. If traveling with young children, the Tadpole playground is a great place to enjoy.

Official Frog Pond website: http://www.bostonfrogpond.com/

Robert Gould Shaw & MA 54th Memorial

At the edge of the Common directly across the street from the State House is Augustus Saint-Gaudens' haunting sculpture memorializing Robert Gould Shaw and the Massachusetts 54th Regiment. Shaw was the only son of a wealthy Boston family. He led the 54th, the first African American unit to be organized to fight in the Civil War. The 1989 epic movie "Glory," with Mathew Broderick, Denzel Washington and Morgan Freeman, memorialized the exploits of the 54th.

Shaw died, along with 74 enlisted men and 3 officers, leading an assault on Fort Wagner, South Carolina in 1863. Sergeant William H. Carney, severely wounded in the assault, saved the regiment's flag from capture. Carney was the first African American to be awarded the Congressional Medal of Honor, the highest military award in the United States.

The monument was unveiled in May of 1897 and was paid for by private donations. It depicts the 54th marching down Beacon Street in 1863 on their way south to join the fight.

Stop 2 - Massachusetts State House

Home to the Mass Legislature and Executive Offices

This State House, designed by Charles Bulfinch, replaced the Old State House (Stop 9) in 1797 and was built on land originally owned by John Hancock.

Free.

Access is via the General Hooker Entrance on the right side of the building. You will need to pass an airport-like security screening to enter the building.

Excellent free tours are offered. It is suggested that you make a reservation, although it is often not required.

Monday-Friday 10-3:30

Official website for tours and information:

http://www.sec.state.ma.us/trs/

617 727-3676

Handicap access: most of the building is accessible via elevators. To enter, use the entrance at Ashburton Park.

Public transportation: Red or Green lines to the Park Street Station.

The tours run about 45 minutes and are worthwhile. Passing through security may take a little time on busy days. Overall, plan about 1.5 hours for your visit.

Web translate section and narration:
http://www.stevestravelguide.com/?p=1264

Background Information

In 1787, four years after the end of the American Revolution, Massachusetts started planning for a new State House. The Old State House (Stop 9) was getting too small and it had too many memories of British authority.

Charles Bulfinch was selected as the architect. The plans were drawn up in 1787, but the land for the project, originally John Hancock's pasture, was not purchased until 1795, two years after Hancock's death.

Building started on July 4th 1795, when, with Samuel Adam and Paul Revere presiding, 15 white horses (one for each state in the union - the original 13 plus Vermont and Kentucky) pulled the cornerstone up the hill.

The red brick building, with its white marble trim, stone steps, and impressive dome, was completed in 1797. The dome is capped with a pine cone, which was placed to honor the lumber industry. What you see today has been expanded several times - the original red brick portion was just 61 feet deep. The wings and the back of the State House were added later.

The dome was originally shingled to combat rot, but in 1802 it was covered with copper, manufactured in Paul Revere's copper rolling factory. Copper from the same factory was also used to coat the hull of the USS Constitution. The gold leaf was not added until 1874.

The dome was painted gray during World War II to keep the city dark during black outs, then re-gilded with 23k gold in 1997. The gold leaf is no thicker than a sheaf of paper, and if rolled together, would be about the size of a pineapple.

Visitors need to enter via the General Hooker Entrance (Hooker was a famous Civil War General) on the right side of the building. The front steps are only used for the President of the United States or foreign heads of state, when soldiers return from war, and when the departing governor takes the "long walk" at the end of his or her term.

Taking a tour inside the State House is highly encouraged, but if you can't take the tour, feel free to visit on your own as there is much to see and it is a beautiful building. One of its more famous tenants is the "Sacred Cod,"

 which honors the importance of the fishing industry to the state. It was given to Massachusetts in 1784 and originally hung in the Old State House. Today it is in the chamber of the House of Representatives. Other artifacts include weapons from the Revolutionary War, a number of paintings by Edward Brodney, Bradford's history of Plimoth (Plymouth), the original Massachusetts Charter, battle flags, and a cannon captured from the British during the War.

The State House is the oldest building on Beacon Hill and sits close to the crest of the hill. When the State House was built, Beacon Hill was considered "the country" and actually consisted of three connected hills - Beacon (Sentry), Cotton (Pemberton) and Mount Vernon (Mount Whoredom). Since that period, Cotton and Mount Vernon were leveled and Beacon was cut down to about 1/2 its original height. The land removed helped fill in areas of the Charles River, Boston Harbor and Back Bay.

Visiting the State House & Acorn Street on Beacon Hill

Stop 3 – Park Street Church

Bastion of Human Rights and Social Justice

Founded in 1809, the Park Street Church was built on the site of original town granary.

    Free
    Tours late June-August, Tuesday - Saturday 9 – 4; year round Sundays
    Website for information:
    http://www.parkstreet.org/
    617-523-3383
    Handicap access is via elevator and requires the staff to be alerted.
    Public Transportation: Red or Green lines to the Park Street Station

Web-translate section and narration:
http://www.stevestravelguide.com/?p=1274

Background Information

The Park Street Church is among the most beautiful in Boston, with its 217 foot steeple visible from many parts of the city. Its congregation originally spun off from the Old South Meeting House (Stop 8).

Park Street Church was designed by Peter Banner in 1809, who was inspired by Christopher Wren's London churches. It held its first service in early 1810. Henry James called it "the most interesting mass of bricks and mortar" in America.

It carries the nickname "Brimstone Corner," which may refer either to the fiery nature of the sermons or to the fact that gunpowder was stored in its crypt during the War of 1812. Brimstone (sulfur) is a major component of gunpowder along with charcoal and saltpeter.

Over the years the Park Street Church has been a bastion of social and missionary work. It was the site of one of America's first Sunday schools (1816), the first prison aid society (1824), and early temperance society meetings (1826). The first missionaries were sent from here to Hawaii (1819). The church was the site of William Lloyd Garrison's first public anti-slavery address in 1829. The song "America" (My Country 'tis of Thee) was sung publicly from its steps for the first time in 1831.

Stop 4 - Granary Burying Ground

Resting Place of Patriots

Founded in 1660, the Granary Burying Ground is the final resting place for three signers of the Declaration of Independence (John Hancock, Samuel Adams and Robert Treat Paine), nine Massachusetts governors, Paul Revere, the Boston Massacre Victims, Ben Franklin's parents and, according to legend, even Mother Goose.

Free
Open daily 9 AM - 5 PM
Official website:
http://www.cityofboston.gov/freedomtrail/granary.asp
617-635-4505
Handicap access is via the entrance at the end of Tremont Place. Go past the main Tremont Street entrance, turn left on Beacon Street and left into the alley at Tremont Place. Enter through the gate on the right at the end of the alley.
No rest rooms.
Public Transportation: Red or Green lines to the Park Street Station.
Plan about 15 minutes to walk through.

Web-translate section and narration:
http://www.stevestravelguide.com/?p=1280

Background Information

The Granary Burying Ground is the third oldest in Boston, behind King's Chapel and Copp's Hill Burying Grounds. It is on land that was once part of Boston Common and takes its name from the town granary that was located next door at the current site of the Park Street Church. There are about 2,300 identifiable graves, but estimates of the actual number of people buried run between 5,000 and 8,000.

You will notice that the graves are nicely laid out in neat rows. This is not the way people were actually buried. They were buried quite haphazardly and often several deep. The stones were moved to their current configuration much later. Therefore, the headstone you are standing before likely has no relation to the body that lies beneath it.

There are three types of graves: the headstone or footstone is the most common. The table tombs look like tables and have the bodies buried in a vault underneath the table stones. The vaults were the most expensive and often favored by wealthy families. They typically hold several bodies even if there is only one name on the vault.

As you enter the graveyard, the first thing you will notice is the large Franklin cenotaph in the center of the cemetery. This obelisk marks the grave of Benjamin Franklin's parents, Josiah and Abiah. Ben Franklin was born in Boston in 1706, but left for Philadelphia when he was 17. He died there in 1790 and that is where his remains are buried. The obelisk is surrounded by several other members of the Franklin family.

Taking a left turn immediately after entering the burying ground, you will find the stone of James Otis Jr. on the right. Otis was one of the most brilliant and important pre-Revolutionary thinkers. Otis was not a revolutionary in the mold of Samuel Adams, but instead remained a loyal British subject.

In 1761, it was Otis who delivered the famous and impassioned four hour legal case that questioned the legality of the Writs of Assistance. John Adams later said that hearing Otis's argument was a critical in influencing him to join the Patriot cause. After 1761, Otis suffered from increasing mental illness and became less influential as a Patriot leader. Otis died in 1783 at age 58.

Proceeding toward the rear of the cemetery, there is a white pillar on the left that marks the grave of John Hancock (1737-1793). This pillar is a replacement for the original monument, which was stolen in the 1800's.

There are many rumors regarding what might have happened to Hancock's remains as the grave remained open for some time when the original marker was stolen. One rumor has asserted that the ring-laden hand that Hancock used to sign the Declaration of Independence was cut off and stolen!

Next to John Hancock's pillar is a stone that reads "Frank, servant to John Hancock, Esq." Frank died in 1771 and, given the absence of a last name, was likely Hancock's slave. It is obvious that Hancock held him in high regard.

At the end of the path is the table tomb of Peter Faneuil (1700-1743). Faneuil was one of Boston's richest merchants and personally paid for the building of Faneuil Hall (Stop 11). Unfortunately, he died of dropsy at only 43 years, only six months after Faneuil Hall was completed.

Proceeding down the rear path towards the center of the cemetery is the square white marble Paul Revere monument. In addition to his famous duties as a messenger for the Patriot cause (he made at least 18 official rides with destinations that included Portsmouth, N.H., New York and Philadelphia, PA), he was a silversmith, dental technician, artist-engraver, entrepreneur, gunpowder maker, engineer, copper magnate, iron and brass forger, bell maker - the list is almost endless. He died in 1818 at the age of 83, a remarkable man. The house Paul Revere lived in at the time of his

Headstone of Paul Revere   1775 ride is Stop 12.

The next grave most tourists visit belongs to Boston's version of Mother Goose. There is conflicting evidence as to who was the original Mother Goose, but this grave is much visited. This Mary Goose was the second wife of Isaac Goose (also known as Vergoose or Vertigoose), who added her own six children to Isaac's ten. She died in 1758 at the age of 92.

Continuing your walk around the edge of the Burying Ground and towards the front, pass the perimeter vault of Robert Treat Paine. Paine was one of the most influential Patriots, serving in the Massachusetts General Court, the Provincial Congress and representing Massachusetts in the Continental Congress. He was one of the 56 signers of the Declaration of Independence. He died in 1814 at the age of 83.

Continuing to the front row, pause before the monument of Samuel Adams, who died in 1803 at the age of 81. Adams was the single most important influencer of the thoughts and actions that led to the American Revolution. There is a statue of Adams behind Faneuil Hall, and a wonderful John Singleton Copley portrait of Adams hangs in the Museum of Fine Arts.

Next to Adams' stone is the memorial for five of the Boston Massacre victims - Samuel Gray, Samuel Maverick, James Caldwell, Crispus Attucks, and Patrick Carr. Also buried here is Christopher Seider, who was killed 11 days before the Massacre by a British customs officer. Seider's murder inflamed the already volatile tensions between the Patriots and the British. After his death, Seider was proclaimed a martyr and Samuel Adams orchestrated his elaborate funeral, with over 2,000 people in attendance.

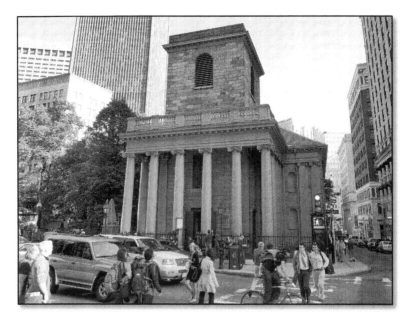

Stop 5 – King's Chapel

First Anglican Church in Boston

This church, built in 1754, was built around the original 1689 building so as not to disturb services. When completed, the original church was broken up and removed through the windows.

Free, but a charge for the Bell & Bones tour (recommended). Wonderful 35 minute music recitals on Tuesday at 12:15, suggested donation $3.

Mon, Thu, Fri. Sat. 10-3*; Tues, Wed 10-11:00, 1-3* Last entry 15 minutes prior to close. Check as the church may be closed due to scheduled or unscheduled services or inclement weather. *=4PM Mem-Labor Day.

Official website: http://www.kings-chapel.org 617-227-2155

Handicap access: there is a 2.5" sill at the entrance, otherwise the building is accessible.

Public Transportation: Red or Green lines to the Park Street Station. Alternative, take the Red or Green lines to Government Center.

Plan 15 minutes to walk through.

Web-translate section and narration:
http://www.stevestravelguide.com/?p=1304

Background Information

Boston's Puritan population was successful in resisting the establishment of a Church of England chapel for many years. Finally, when King James II came to power in 1685, he ordered the new Governor, Sir Edmund Andros, to establish one. Andros took charge after arrival in 1686.

First, Andros had to find space for the Anglican congregation to hold services. Finding the Puritans unwilling to share meeting house space, he demanded the keys to Old South Meeting House. The Old South congregation then had to wait outside on Sundays until the Anglican services were finished before they could hold their own services.

As the Puritans were unwilling to sell land for an Anglican chapel, Andros seized the land from a corner of the town's burying ground by eminent domain. The original wooden King's Chapel was ready in 1689, and the Old South congregation returned to their normal service schedule.

The current granite chapel was started in 1749 when the original became too small. The new chapel was built around the old wooden one so as not to disturb the services. Puritan and Bostonian law also indicated that if the walls were knocked down, the land would revert back to the Puritans. When the new chapel was finished, the old one was dismantled and tossed out through the windows. It opened for services in 1754.

As the first Anglican Church (Church of England) in Boston, it was recipient of many lavish gifts from the British monarchy. King William III and Queen Mary II (1689 - 1702) sent money, communion silver, altar cloths, carpets and cushions. Queen Anne (1702 - 1714) gave vestments and red cushions. King George III (1760 - 1820) donated more silver communion pieces. The silver pieces vanished when half of the parishioners fled (they were Royalists) when the British left Boston after the Siege of Boston was lifted in 1776.

The chapel was designed by America's first professional architect, Peter Harrison. Interestingly, Harrison never saw the building or its location. The congregation provided the requirements by letter and Harrison sent back completed plans. He worked strictly out of his Newport R.I office.

The chapel still contains many original details. The communion table was built in 1694. The box pews are original as are the hand-carved Corinthian columns. The Wineglass pulpit dates from 1717 and is the oldest pulpit in continuous use on the same site in America. The organ is a replica of the 1754 instrument, which was the first organ to be permanently installed in any church in British America. The bell was crafted by Paul Revere in 1816; the last he ever made, it weighs 2,347 pounds.

In 1785, the congregation adopted a new theology and became the first Unitarian church in America, some 40 years before the Unitarian church became a formal body. Today the church is combination of Unitarian with some liturgy adopted from Anglican Book of Common Prayers.

JOHN WINTHROP 1588 - 1649
1ST GOVERNOR of MASSACHUSETTS
JOHN WINTHROP the YOUNGER 1606 - 1676
1ST GOVERNOR of CONNECTICUT
MAJ. GEN. FITZ JOHN WINTHROP 1638 - 1707
GOVERNOR of CONNECTICUT
MAJ. GEN. WAIT STILL WINTHROP 1642 - 1717
CHIEF JUSTICE of MASSACHUSETTS
ADAM WINTHROP 1647 - 1700
COLONEL ADAM WINTHROP 1676 - 1743
PROF. JOHN WINTHROP L.L.D. 1714 - 1779
ANN WINTHROP 1756 - 1789
WIFE of DAVID SEARS

Stop 5a - King's Chapel Burying Ground

Oldest Burying Ground in Boston

King's Chapel Burying Ground is the final resting place for Boston's earliest settlers including the family of William Dawes (the other rider on Paul Revere's Midnight Ride) and John Winthrop (the Puritan leader at the founding of Boston in 1630 and the first governor).

Free
Open daily 9 - 5
617-635-4505
Plan about 10 minutes to walk through.

Web-translate section and narration:
http://www.stevestravelguide.com/?p=1307

Background Information

King's Chapel Burying Ground is Boston's oldest. It was originally the vegetable garden of Sir Isaac Johnson, which also extended to the area surrounding Old City Hall (just behind the Chapel and Burying Ground). Sir Isaac died within a year of his arrival in Boston and was buried in the garden. It has no association with King's Chapel, which was not built until 50 years after the Burying Ground was established.

There are many more people buried here than the headstones suggest - often they are buried four deep and sometimes standing up. Also, as with the other early Burying Grounds, the headstones have been moved into more orderly rows, so a headstone may not represent the actual burial site.

The burying ground was full by 1660, which means that none of the famous Revolutionary-era personalities are buried here.

There are, however, many internees who played important roles in Boston's history. The most historically significant is the memorial for John Winthrop (1587 - 1649), who is buried along with his family. Winthrop was the leading figure in the founding of the Massachusetts Bay Colony (the trading company that owned the rights to the Massachusetts settlements). He led the Puritan's 1630 migration from England that led to Boston's founding, and he was the first (and a twelve term) governor.

The oldest headstone here, and the oldest remaining in Boston, belongs to William Paddy, who died in 1658. The most famous stone, located just inside the entry gate, is that of Joseph Tapping, who died in 1678. Tapping's headstone shows Father Time battling with a skeleton over the eventuality of death. Many consider this to be among the most beautiful in Boston.

You will also find the graves of Mary Chilton, who, according to legend, was the first Pilgrim to touch land in America., the family of William Dawes (the "other" rider on Paul Revere's Ride), and Elizabeth Pain, who inspired Hester Prynne in Nathaniel Hawthorne's "The Scarlet Letter."

The ventilator shaft on the right side of the Burying Ground, close to King's Chapel, dates from 1898. It is a relic of the first subway system built in America.

Stop 6 - Boston Latin, Franklin Statue, & Old City Hall

First Public School in America

Site of the original Boston Latin School, the Ben Franklin statue (the oldest portrait statue in the US), and Old City Hall (served as Boston City Hall from 1865 until 1969).

Free - everything is outside

Public Transportation: Red, Silver or Orange lines to Downtown Crossing.

Plan for 5-10 minutes to see the statues and plaques.

Web-translate section and narration:
http://www.stevestravelguide.com/?p=1315

Background Information

Just down the street from King's Chapel (behind the Chapel), there is a mosaic embedded in the pavement. The mosaic, by Lilli Anne Killen Rosenberg, represents the original Boston Latin School, founded in April of 1635. The actual school was located at the site of the Franklin statue.

For the school's first 10 years, classes were held in the headmaster's house. The first school-specific building was completed in 1645. It was razed in 1745 to make way for the expanded King's Chapel.

Boston Latin was the first public school in America. It was modeled after the Free Grammar School of the Puritans' ancestral home of

Boston, Lincolnshire, England. Boston Latin was to provide a foundation for a who's who of American revolutionary thought, including Samuel Adams, Benjamin Franklin (a non-graduate), John Hancock, and Robert Treat Paine.

The Puritans were highly committed to education, not the least so that their children would be able to read the Bible. The commitment to education was so strong that a law was passed in 1647 that required the establishment of elementary schools in all surrounding towns of 50 or more families. Rich or poor could attend, but typically students needed to pay for firewood with cash or by trade. African Americans and girls were not welcome in colonial times. The girls were tutored at home.

The following year, in 1636, Harvard College was founded in nearby Cambridge. Harvard's goal was not only to train students for the ministry, but also for other higher pursuits including law and medicine. Harvard's Revolutionary-era alumni not only included most of the Boston Latin graduates, but also James Otis, Jr., John Adams, and even some prominent Loyalists, such as the English Governor at the time of the Boston Tea Party, Thomas Hutchinson.

Just behind the mosaic on the other side of the cast iron fence is the beautiful Old City Hall. It is in the Second Empire style and was started in 1862, completed in 1865. It was home of the city of Boston's city council from 1865 until 1969, when the new city hall on City Hall Plaza was completed. It now houses private offices.

The brass donkey in front of City Hall represents the Democratic Party. The two brass footprints in the pavement in front of the donkey invite you to "Stand Here In Opposition." The footprints have an image of an elephant – representing the Republican Party. You can stand or sit where you feel most comfortable.

The Province Steps (Province House)

For a brief detour, cross the street from Old City Hall and walk up Province Street. About 3/4 the way up the block on the right there are a few granite steps. The steps are all that remain of the Province House, and originally led from the back of the mansion into its formal gardens. The Province House (1679–1864) was the official residence of the Royal Governors until the American Revolution. The restaurant right above the steps is Café Marliave, the oldest Italian restaurant in Boston, which dates from 1875.

Stop 7 - Old Corner Bookstore

Leading US Publisher 1833-64

Built in 1711 after the original house burned, under Ticknor and Fields, it was the nation's leading publisher and produced works by Longfellow, Stowe, Hawthorne, Emerson, and Dickens.

It now houses a Chipotle Mexican Grill.
Web-translate section and narration:
http://www.stevestravelguide.com/?p=1318

Background Information

The original house on this site belonged to Quaker Anne Hutchinson, who was banished from Boston in 1637. That house survived until 1711, when it burned in the first "Great Fire," which consumed a major part of Boston, including Boston's Town House (at the site of the current Old State House, Stop 9) and the Old Meeting House (Boston's first Meeting House).

Soon after that fire, the current house was built by Dr. Thomas Crease to serve as both his residence and an apothecary. After several incarnations as a dry-goods store, residence and another apothecary, it became a bookstore and printing shop in 1828 when it was leased to Carter and Handee.

Five years later, in 1832, it was leased to publisher William Ticknor, who took in James T. Fields as his partner. Fields began editing a magazine called the *Atlantic Monthly* – printed on a printing press that was driven by two Canadian horses. The *Atlantic Monthly* is still published today.

The company's greatest legacy was their development of the royalty system for authors. With this innovation, authors were able to share in the proceeds from their books sales for the first time. Prior to this, publishers purchased book rights for a set fee.

Ticknor and Fields was the nation's leading publisher 1833-1864. Their authors included Henry Wadsworth Longfellow, Harriet Beecher Stowe, Nathaniel Hawthorne, Ralph Waldo Emerson, John Greenleaf Whittier, Oliver Wendell Holmes, Sr., Charles Dickens, and Louisa May Alcott.

During this period Ticknor and Fields was the regular meeting place for all the great writers of New England. It became known as "Parnassus Corner," a reference to the mountain home of the Twelve Muses of Greek mythology. The building was restored in 1960.

The Irish Famine Memorial

The Irish Famine Memorial commemorates the Great Irish Famine, which took place between 1845 and 1852. Many Irishmen and women immigrated to Boston during the famine, settling originally in Boston's North End.

The Stage in Faneuil Hall's Great Hall

Stop 8 - Old South Meeting House

Home of Rebel Dissension

As Boston's largest building in the Colonial period, Old South was the site of many important gatherings and became the emblematic home of the Patriot cause.

Admission $6, seniors & and students $5, Children (6-18) $1 - AAA/MBTA Charlie Card discount. WGBH members, 2 for 1 admission.

Open Daily, 10-4. April 1 - October 31 9:30-5; November 1 - March 31 10-4

Closed Thanksgiving, Christmas Eve Day, Christmas, and New Year's Day
Official website:
http://www.oldsouthmeetinghouse.org/
617-482-6439
Handicap access: wheelchair accessible, listening devices available
Public transportation: State Street (Blue/Orange Lines), Government Center (Green Line) and Downtown Crossing (Red Line).

Plan about 1/2 hour to view the interior and the exhibits.

Web-translate section and narration:
http://www.stevestravelguide.com/?p=1321

Background Information

The Old South congregation was created when a group of dissenters split off from the First Church in 1669. Their original meeting house, a simple cedar sided building, was built on a part of what was the corn and potato patch of John Winthrop - the first Puritan leader. After Winthrop died, the land was owned by influential preacher John Norton. It was donated to the congregation by John's widow, Mary.

The original meeting house was the site of Benjamin Franklin's baptism, which took place on a wintry night in January of 1706. The first meeting house was torn down in early 1729. The current structure, based on Christopher Wren's work in London, was dedicated in April of 1730.

The new meeting house was the largest building in Boston and was host to many significant meetings. As the conflicts with England amplified during pre-Revolutionary years, it became known in London for its role as a key place for Colonial protests. Almost every significant Patriot leader held court here - including James Otis, Samuel Adams, John Hancock, and Dr. Joseph Warren.

Perhaps the most famous meetings associated with Old South are those that preceded the Boston Tea Party. At the final meeting, over 5,000 townspeople (1/3 of Boston's population at the time) heard Samuel Adams say "Gentlemen, this meeting can do nothing more to save the country." Legend has it that this was the signal for about 100 Patriots dressed as Native Americans to march to Boston Harbor and begin the Boston Tea Party.

Old South was such a symbol of Patriot dissension that during Boston's occupation during the Siege of Boston (1775-1776), British troops ripped out the pews and pulpit and used them for fuel. It was filled with dirt and turned it into a riding school for the British Cavalry. After the war, it took almost eight years to raise the money to refurbish the Meeting House to make it usable as a place of worship.

Old South was almost destroyed in the Great Fire of 1872. Soon after the fire, it was sold and the congregation moved to Copley Square in Back Bay. Today it is a museum and one of the most interesting stops on the Freedom Trail.

Benjamin Franklin's Birthplace

The site of Benjamin Franklin's birthplace is just across the street from Old South at the location of the current 17 Milk Street. Ben was the eighth child of the ten children of Josiah Franklin and his second wife, Abiah. (Overall, he was the fifteenth of seventeen for Josiah.) Today it is an office building.

The Old State House & Boston Massacre Site

Stop 9 - Old State House

Oldest Public Building in Boston (1713)

The Old State House was the site of the British government offices until they left after the Siege of Boston in 1776, and the state legislature until 1798. It was the site of many important Revolutionary-era events

Official website:

http://www.RevolutionaryBoston.org (617) 720-1713

The current building replaced the first Town House, built on this site between 1657-68, burned down in the Great Fire of 1711.

It is now the home of the Bostonian Society and houses an excellent museum and programs.

Open daily, 9 - 5, January 9 - 4, July and August 9- 6

Closed New Year's, Thanksgiving, and Christmas

Admission $6, Seniors & Students $5, Children (6-18) $1.

The Old State House is not considered wheelchair accessible. There are plans to address this, but please call to confirm.

Public transportation: Orange or Blue lines to State Street. Alternative, Green line to Government Center, or Red line to Downtown Crossing.

The talks given by museum personnel are excellent and run 20-30 minutes - covering subjects such as the Boston Massacre and Old State House History. The museum has interesting collections. Plan at least an hour for your visit.

Web-translate section and narration:

http://www.stevestravelguide.com/?p=1328

Background Information

Boston's first official town hall, called the Town House, was started in 1657 and dedicated in 1658. It was enabled when Robert Keayne willed £300 for a Town House with stipulations not only to size and construction, but also that it would contain a marketplace, a library, and serve as the home for the Ancient and Honorable Artillery Company, of which he was the commander. Keayne's bequest was doubled by over 100 "Townesmen," enabling the Town House to be built.

The first Town House served for the next 53 years until it burned down in the Great Fire of 1711. Within two years, the current Old State House was built. This building was gutted by fire in 1747 and reconstructed over the next three years.

The Old State House was to serve as the location for British Government offices until the British left Boston in 1776. In addition to the meeting chamber of the Royal Governor, the Massachusetts Assembly and the Courts of Suffolk County and the Massachusetts Supreme Judicial Courts met here.

The Old State House was the site of many significant events leading up to the revolution, including James Otis's impassioned argument against the Writs of Assistance in 1761. In 1770, the Boston Massacre took place just in front of the building.

Official proclamations were read from the balcony overlooking State Street (it was called King Street before the Revolution). On July 18, 1776, the Declaration of Independence was read from the balcony to a crowd of excited Bostonians. Soon after hearing the Declaration, the lion and unicorn, symbols of the British monarchy, were torn down. They were replaced during the building's renovation in 1882.

After the Revolution, the Old State House continued to operate as the seat of Massachusetts government until the new State House was completed in 1798. The state then wanted to sell the building and share the money with the town. The town rejected the plan and instead purchased sole title.

The building was subsequently rented to a wide variety of businesses including cobblers, harness makers, and wine vendors. A bank tried to purchase it in 1822. For a period between 1830 and 1844 it became a Boston City Hall.

By the 1870's it was dilapidated and an eyesore. The city of Chicago offered to buy it, tear it down and move it to Lake Michigan "for all America to revere." Shamed by the proposal, in 1881 the Boston Antiquarian Club was formed, later incorporating as the Bostonian Society. The Society persuaded the city to save and restore the building.

Today, the Bostonian Society operates an excellent museum that features talks and tours. The museum displays artifacts from the Revolutionary period that include many of John Hancock's personal possessions. It is a worthwhile stop.

Stop 10 – Boston Massacre Site

This was the site of the Boston Massacre, which occurred on March 5, 1770. The Massacre took place after an unfortunate chain of events led British soldiers to fire on an angry Boston mob, killing five and wounding six. Although hardly a massacre (most of the soldiers were later acquitted of blame), it was to be an important propaganda event in provoking Colonial unrest.

There is a plaque on the ground just beneath the balcony of the Old State House that marks the site.

This is a walk-by with a photo opportunity. Web-translate this section and narration: http://www.stevestravelguide.com/?p=1332

Stop 11 – Faneuil Hall

The Cradle of Liberty

Given to the town by wealthy merchant Peter Faneuil in 1742, the Hall was host to many important Revolutionary-era meetings and events including speeches by James Otis and Samuel Adams, the establishment of the first Committee of Correspondence, and the first meeting to protest the tea tax that led to the Boston Tea Party.

Free The first floor is home to the National Park Service Visitor Center.

Open daily, 9-5 except during events; Ranger talks every thirty minutes.

Official website: http://www.nps.gov/bost/historyculture/fh.htm

617-242-5642

Handicap ramp and elevators are at the south side door near the Bostix booth. Enter through the Visitor Center.

Restrooms are in the basement and 2nd floor.

Public transportation: Green or Blue line to Government Center.

The Ancient and Honorable Artillery Company, the oldest chartered military organization in North America, has a museum on the 3rd floor. Website: http://www.ahac.us.com/

Be sure to attend the Ranger talk if your time permits. Allow at least 1/2 hour for your visit. The Quincy Market area next to Faneuil Hall is a good place to shop, eat, and wander. In nice weather there are street performers and it is one of the most visited areas in Boston.

Web-translate section and narration:

http://www.stevestravelguide.com/?p=1338

Background Information

As you approach Faneuil Hall from the Old State House, you will see a bronze statue of Samuel Adams (pictured above). This represents Adams as he defiantly confronted British Governor Hutchinson after the Boston Massacre. Before being moved here, the statue stood in Adams Square, which was demolished to create Government Center.

At the base of the statue, there are a number of markings in the pavement that represents the harbor's water line in 1630. All the land from here to the current harbor has been filled-in.

Faneuil Hall was given to Boston by Peter Faneuil (1700-1743). Peter was the son of Benjamin and Anne Faneuil, wealthy French Huguenots (Protestants) who, along with Peter's uncle Andrew, fled from religious persecution in 1685. Peter's father died when he was 18. Uncle Andrew, a shrewd merchant and real estate investor, became one of the richest men in New England.

On his own, Peter became a successful merchant running a triangular trading operation shipping slaves from Africa to the West Indies in exchange for the molasses used to make New England rum. Boston and New England was the world's largest rum producer during the colonial period.

In addition to his own success, Peter inherited a significant fortune from his Uncle Andrew. It is interesting to note that his Uncle's estate came with the stipulation that Peter never marry. Peter accepted the conditions and remained a bachelor.

Uncle Andrew died in 1738 when Peter was thirty eight. Unfortunately, Peter was only able to enjoy his increased fortune for five more years as he

Faneuil Hall & Quincy Market in *1838* (Note the site of the Waterline)

was to die of dropsy (edema) when he was only 43. He did live well during his remaining time, living up to the name of one of his ships – The Jolly Bachelor. He left behind a cellar full of fine wine, cheese and beer.

The town's decision to allow Faneuil Hall to be built was not without controversy. Even though Boston was a major seaport by the early 1700s, it did not have a large central market. Although a central market was a normal feature of English towns and would simplify things for most merchants, many vendors opposed developing the market. They believed that if their stalls were centrally located, it would lead to increased price competition.

In 1740, Peter proposed to build the central market for the town at his own expense. His proposal was not universally popular and passed by only seven votes, 367 to 360.

The original design had stalls facing out on all four sides - waterfront, fish market, hay market and sheep market. To help appease the opposition, Faneuil added a meeting hall above the market space.

Work began September 1740 and was completed in September 1742, only six months before Peter's death. The first public use of Faneuil Hall was for Peter's funeral, in March 1743. The building suffered a major fire in 1761. When it was rebuilt in 1762, the meeting hall was enlarged.

Faneuil Hall received a major expansion between 1805 and 1806 based on Charles Bulfinch's design. Both its height and width were doubled, and the cupola was moved to the opposite end of the building. The open arcades that served as the market areas were enclosed. Between 1898 and 1899 the building's combustible materials were replaced.

One original fixture of the building is the grasshopper weather vane on top of the cupola. This was created by Shem Drowne, and is from copper and gold leaf with glass doorknobs for eyes. It was stolen in 1974, but was later found hidden in the cupola's eaves wrapped in some old flags.

The grasshopper became such a Boston icon that it was used during the War of 1812 to screen for spies. If someone claimed to be from Boston and they did not know about the weathervane, they had to be a spy.

As a political venue, Faneuil Hall has more than earned the name "Cradle of Liberty". During the Revolutionary period, it was the site of many important political events. In May of 1764 it hosted the first protest over the Sugar Act. Rallies were held here against the Stamp Act (1765), the Townshend Acts (1767), and the landing of British Troops that were sent to quell the associated disturbances (1768) – which ultimately led to the Boston Massacre in 1770. The funeral for Boston Massacre victims was held here.

Led by Samuel Adams, in 1772 the first Committee of Correspondence was established here. In 1773, Faneuil Hall hosted the first of the meetings to protest the tea tax. These meetings were so well attended they were moved to the Old South Meeting House.

During the British occupation in 1775 and 1776, it was a barracks for troops, then later a theater. In one incident, British General Burgoyne's theatrical farce *The Blockade of Boston* was being performed at Faneuil Hall when it was interrupted by a small Patriot attack on Charlestown. It seems that the Patriots had learned of the play and precisely timed their attack to disturb the British performance.

After the war, Faneuil Hall continued to serve as a center of political activity. In the 1800s, it was a key rallying point in the anti-slavery movement, hosting abolitionists such as Wendell Phillips, William Lloyd Garrison and Frederick Douglas. Jefferson Davis, later president of Confederacy, spoke here in defense of slavery.

Faneuil Hall was also host to events in support of the women's rights movement and temperance. It was the sight of John Fitzgerald Kennedy's final campaign speech, made just prior to his election to the presidency in 1960. This tradition continues as the Hall hosts political debates and is a frequent campaign stop for both local and national politicians.

On third floor is the Armory Museum of the Ancient and Honorable Artillery Company. The Ancient & Honorable Artillery Company is the oldest chartered military organization in North America. Today largely ceremonial, it was founded in 1637 to protect the colony against Indian attack. The Armory, located here since it moved from the Town House (the predecessor to the Old State House) in 1746, holds relics from all periods of American history.

Quincy Market / Faneuil Hall Marketplace

When Boston incorporated as a city in 1822, the market around Faneuil Hall was not large enough to meet the city's needs. Under the leadership of Boston's second Mayor, Josiah Quincy III (a statue of Quincy stands outside of Old City Hall - Stop 6), Quincy Market was built to provide the additional market capacity. It was completed in 1826 and used initially as a foodstuff and produce shopping center. At the time of its construction, it was at the harbor's edge. The North Market and South Market buildings, which stand on either side of Quincy Market, were built in the mid 1800's.

By the middle 1970's the whole area had deteriorated. It was revitalized as part of the preparations for the United States Bicentennial in 1976. Today, it is one of the busiest tourist destinations in Boston.

The Blackstone Block and the Holocaust Memorial

As you proceed down the Freedom Trail from Faneuil Hall (a left out of the front door), you will cross North Street and walk down Union Street towards the North End and the next Stop, the Paul Revere House. The intersection of North and Union Street begins the Blackstone Block – bounded by Union, North, Hanover, and Blackstone Streets. These streets were among the first streets to be laid out in Boston, and date from the 1600s.

On the grass mall just to left of Union Street, you will see the six glass towers of the Holocaust Memorial, established by survivors of the Nazi concentration camps. Each of the six towers represents one of the six primary Nazi concentration camps.

The towers are set on a black granite path, and glow at night. Each tower rises over a black chamber that emanates smoke from charred embers, creating an almost spiritual feeling. Six million numbers, suggesting the tattoos that were cut into those that perished during the Holocaust, are etched in glass.

This is a haunting and moving reminder of one of the greatest tragedies of our time.

You now cross Union Street from the Holocaust Memorial. The Union Oyster House on your right. The Union Oyster House is the oldest operating restaurant in the United States.

The Freedom Trail now winds down Marshall Street towards the North End. Marshall Street is one of the oldest and most authentically colonial streets remaining in Boston. On the right, past the Green Dragon, is the Ebenezer Hancock House.

Faneuil Hall's Great Hall

The Ebenezer Hancock House was built in 1767 by John Hancock's uncle. John inherited it and gave it to his brother Ebenezer, who became the deputy paymaster of the Continental Army during the Revolution.

The Boston Stone, directly across from Ebenezer's house, has been a landmark since 1737. A painter brought the stone from England to grind pigments prior to 1700. According to legend, it served as the "zero milestone," used for measuring the distance to Boston – e.g., "20 miles to Boston" would mean 20 miles to this stone. The dome of the State House on Beacon Hill is Boston's current zero milestone.

Proceed down Marshall Street, cross Hanover Street, and take a right to the North End. On Fridays and Saturdays you will pass through the Haymarket open-air market. There is a huge variety of fruits, vegetables, meats and seafood - all at bargain prices. Buy some berries to go with the pastries that will tempt you in the North End. Be careful of pickpockets.

Now cross through the Rose Kennedy Greenway to the North End. The Greenway is a series of parks that wind through the city covering the site of the Big Dig. An elevated highway used to bar the entrance to the North End (the trellis you see is at the height of the old highway). The Big Dig moved the highway (Route 93) underneath the city. So right now, you will be walking over Route 93.

Stop 12 – Paul Revere House

Oldest Building in Boston c. 1680

This was home to the Revere family at the time of Paul's famous ride to alert the Patriots of the British march on Lexington and Concord.

Adults $3.5; Seniors and College Students $3; Children (5-17) $1

Open Daily April 15 - October 31 - 9:30 - 5:15, November 1 - April 14 - 9:30 - 4:15, Closed on Mondays in January, February and March. Closed on Thanksgiving, Christmas Day and New Year's Day.

Official website:

http://www.paulreverehouse.org/

(617) 523-2338

Handicap accessible first floor (about 1/2 of the small museum). Ask at the ticket booth for a temporary ramp.

No restrooms

Public transportation: Green or Orange line to Haymarket Station.

Interesting old house with knowledgeable guides, the last of its type in Boston. Some Revere relics. It is very small. Photography inside prohibited.

Plan 1/4-1/2 hour

Web-translate section and narration:
http://www.stevestravelguide.com/?p=1346

Background Information

The Paul Revere House in North Square is the oldest remaining building in Boston. It was built on the ashes of the Second Church of Boston's (Old North Meeting House) parsonage, which was the home to Increase Mather and his family (including his son Cotton). The parsonage burned in 1676.

The original house dates from about 1680. Its first owner was Robert Howard. By the time Revere purchased the house in 1770 it had undergone significant changes with the front roof line being raised in the popular Georgian style and a partial third story added.

Revere moved in with his first wife, Sarah, his mother and five of his children. Sarah bore him a total of eight children, and he had another eight with his second wife, Rachel. Revere's silversmith shop was a couple of blocks away.

Revere owned the house until 1800, but likely moved out as early as 1780. After he sold the house, it served as a tenement with its ground floor remodeled for use as shops.

The house was purchased by Revere's great-grandson in 1902 to prevent its demolition. It then underwent restoration to an approximation of its 1700 appearance, opening in 1908 as one of the earliest historic house museums in the United States.

During the renovation, the roof line was restored to its original pitch, but without its gable. Despite the renovation, ninety percent of the house is original including the foundation and inner wall material, some doors, window frames, and portions of the flooring, foundation, inner wall material and raftering. All the glass has been replaced. Inside, there are several pieces of furniture believed to have belonged to the Reveres.

Adjacent to the Paul Revere house is the brick Pierce-Hichborn House, built about 1711 in the Georgian style. It was owned by Nathaniel Hichborn, a boat builder and cousin of Revere's. It is also a nonprofit museum operated by the Paul Revere Memorial Association.

North Square, North Meeting House & Garden Court Street

The North Square is directly across the street from the Paul Revere house. It was the center of the North End life and commerce during Colonial times and the site of some of the town's most impressive mansions.

It was also the site for the North Meeting House (Boston's Second Church), which was first built in 1649, burned down in

Plaque at the site of the Hutchinson Mansion on Garden Court Street

1673, and rebuilt the following year. It was used by the British for firewood during the winter of 1775-76 during the Siege of Boston.

Just around the corner from North Square is Garden Court Street. This was the site of the Clark-Frankland and Thomas Hutchinson mansions. Rose Fitzgerald (Kennedy), the mother of President John F. Kennedy, was born at 2 Garden Court Street in 1890.

For more on North Square, see the chapter The North End.

St. Stephen's, Paul Revere Mall & Clough House

The Freedom Trail from Paul Revere's house goes left down Prince Street and right on Hanover Street. Down Hanover Street, just before crossing to enter Paul Revere Mall, you will pass St. Stephen's Church.

Saint Stephen's is the last remaining Charles Bulfinch designed church in Boston. It was completed in 1804 as the New North Congregational Church. It became Unitarian in 1813, and in 1862 was sold to the Roman Catholic Diocese of Boston and renamed St. Stephen's.

Crossing Hanover Street, you enter the Paul Revere Mall. The iconic statue you encounter (also on the cover of the Guide and at the start of the North End chapter) is by Cyrus Dallin. Dallin was a famous sculptor that worked in the nearby town of Arlington, MA.

The Paul Revere Mall, also known as The Prado by locals, was created in 1933. It is a brick passage and park that leads from Hanover Street to the Old North Church. The mall walls are lined with bronze plaques that commemorate famous North End residents.

At the end of the Mall, just before the stairs up to the Old North Church, is the Clough House, which dates from 1712. One of the oldest homes remaining in Boston, it was home to Ebenezer Clough, a master mason who helped build Old North Church. This is representative of many houses that once made up this neighborhood. The house

Clough House with Edes & Gill Printing Museum just outside Old North Church

features a small, but excellent historic printing museum, The Printing Office of Edes & Gill, that is worth visiting – check to see if it is open. http://bostongazette.org/.

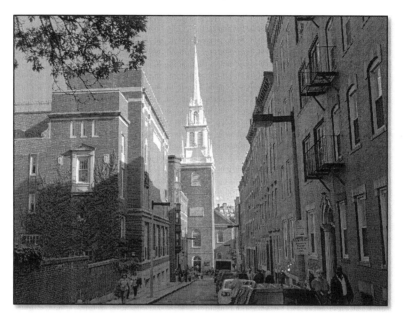

Stop 13 – Old North Church

The Steeple that Started the Revolution

In April, 1775, it was the sight of the hanging lanterns that notified Patriots in Charlestown that the British were leaving "two if by sea" prior to Paul Revere's Midnight Ride and the Battles of Lexington and Concord.

Free (donation, includes self-guided tour) The worthwhile Behind-the-Scenes Tour visits the crypt and bell tower: $5, adult; $3 senior; $4 youth

Open: January–February: 10–4pm, Tues–Sunday; March–May: 9-5 daily; June–October: 9–6 daily; November–December: 10–5 daily

Sunday services 9 and 11 AM

Official website:

http://oldnorth.com/

617-523-6676

Handicap access - there is a 1/2" step at entrance to church; gift shop limited.

No restrooms in the Church

Public transportation: Green or Orange line to Haymarket Station.

Plan about 15 minutes to walk through

Excellent gift store next to the Church

Web-translate section and narration:
http://www.stevestravelguide.com/?p=1352

Background Information

Old North Church, officially known as Christ Church, was begun in 1723 and took twenty-two years to complete. It is the oldest church remaining in Boston. On April 18, 1775 its place in history was cemented when Sexton Robert Newman climbed the steeple and hung the two lanterns that signaled to Patriots watching from Charlestown that the British were marching on Lexington and Concord "by sea".

Old North was the second Anglican Church in Boston, after King's Chapel. As an Anglican Church, the majority of its congregation was loyal to the British King and the membership included the Royal Governor. The King gave Old North its silver and a bible.

The fact that this is an Anglican Church makes its place in American history even more extraordinary as it made the use of the Church by Revere and Newman extremely risky. After hanging the lanterns, Newman had to escape out a window. (The original window through which he left the church was bricked up in 1815. It was rediscovered during restoration work in 1989.) Paul Revere was never a church member as he was a Congregationalist. He did, however, work here as a bell ringer.

Old North was modeled after the work of Sir Christopher Wren in London, perhaps using St. Andrews-by-the-Wardrobe in Blackfriars, London as the model. St. Andrews-by-the-Wardrobe was destroyed by German bombs during World War II, but has since been rebuilt.

The original steeple was destroyed in a storm in 1804 and Charles Bulfinch designed the replacement, which stood until Hurricane Carol in 1954. The current steeple uses design elements from both the original and the Bulfinch version. The church steeple now stands 175 feet (53 m) tall, some sixteen feet lower than the original. At its tip, however, is the original weather vane.

The church bells, the oldest in America, came from England and date from 1744. They were restored in 1894 and again in 1975. They ring regularly, and are beautiful - check the website for the bell ringing schedule.

Many of the church details are original. The high box pews were purchased by congregation members in a manner similar to the way season tickets to sporting events are purchased today - buy first in the back and trade up when a better seat opens up. The pews high walls are designed to retain the warmth of hot coals or bricks placed on the floor. The chandeliers are from England.

The organ, built in 1759, still has some original components and is used. The clock was built by some of the parishioners in 1726. To the left of the pulpit there is a lifelike bust of George Washington that dates from 1815. During his visit in 1824, the Marquis de Lafayette, a key aid of Washington, commented on the extremely lifelike nature of the bust.

Old North's basement holds 1,100 bodies buried in 37 crypts. It was used 1732-1853, each tomb is sealed with a wooden or slate door - many doors still covered by plaster the city ordered in the 1850s.

Old North as seen from City Hall Plaza

The founding rector of the church, Timothy Cutler, was buried right under the altar. Also buried under the church is British Marine Major John Pitcairn, who was mortally wounded at the Battle of Bunker Hill and entombed with many others killed in that battle.

Stop 14 – Copp's Hill Burying Ground

Site of British Battery During Battle of Bunker Hill

Founded in 1659, Copp's Hill's permanent residents include the Puritan ministers Increase and Cotton Mather, Robert Newman (the patriot who hung the lanterns that signaled "two if by sea" in Old North Church), and Prince Hall, the father of Black Freemasonry.

Free - public park Closed as it gets dark Official website:
http://www.cityofboston.gov/parks/hbgi/CoppsHill.asp

Handicap access limited as it is up a steep hill from Old North Church and there are several steep granite steps to climb in order to enter the burying ground. No restrooms

Public transportation: Green or Orange line to North Station.

Plan 10-15 minutes to walk through and view the grave sites.

Web-translate section and narration:
http://www.stevestravelguide.com/?p=1357

Background Information

Copp's Hill Burying Ground, the second oldest in Boston, was founded in 1659. It takes its name from William Copp, the North End shoemaker who was the original owner of the land. The hill is the highest in the North End and originally was the sight of windmills, the source of its original name of Windmill Hill. The burying ground was extended several times as the need increased. The earliest grave markers date to 1661.

On the Snow Hill Street side are the many unmarked graves of the African Americans who lived in the "New Guinea" community at the foot of the hill. In addition to the graves, there are 272 tombs, most of which bear inscriptions that are still legible.

Among the Bostonians buried here are the family of the original owner, William Copp, as well as Robert Newman (the Sexton of the Old North Church who hung the "two if by sea" signal lanterns). Also here is Prince Hall along with many unmarked graves of African Americans who lived on Copp's Hill. Prince Hall was one of the most influential free black leaders in the late 1700s. Hall is known for his work for education rights, as an early abolitionist, and as the father of Black Freemasonry.

The most historically significant memorial is the Mather Tomb, the final resting place for Increase (1639-1723) and his son Cotton Mather (1663-1728). Both Mathers were powerful and politically active ministers of the Old North Meeting House (Boston's Second Church), which was in North Square by the Paul Revere House. They were directly involved in the hysteria surrounding the Salem witch trials which damaged their reputations.

When the British occupied the city during the Siege of Boston, in 1775-1776, Copp's Hill Burying Ground was used for target practice. You can still see impact marks from British musket balls, particularly on the headstone of Captain Daniel Malcom. There's even one in the eye of the skull!

Copp's Hill was also the site of British cannons that were mounted to protect the harbor. During the Battle of Bunker Hill, these cannons were used to bombard Charlestown prior to the assaults. You can see the Bunker Hill Monument and the USS Constitution from the back of the Burying Ground.

Narrowest House

Diagonally across the street from the Burying Ground entrance is the narrowest house in Boston. It is 10.4 feet (3.16 m) at its widest, it tapers to 9.2 feet (2.82 m) at the back. It was allegedly built as a "spite house" a little after 1874.

Stop 15 – USS Constitution

Undefeated in 33 Fights

USS Constitution, or "Old Ironsides," is the oldest commissioned warship afloat in the world.

Free admission, but visitors must show a valid ID and pass through security to visit the ship and enter through the National Parks Service Visitor Center. The Visitor Center has an introductory film and interesting exhibits that cover the Navy Yard and the Constitution.

Nov. 1- March 31 Tues-Sun 10-4; April 1-Sept. 30 Tues-Sun 10-6; Oct. 1- Oct. 31 Tues-Sunday 10-4; Closed for Thanksgiving, Christmas and New Years

A wait is usually required to take the worthwhile USS Constitution tour.

Official National Park Service phone & website: (617) 242-5601

http://www.nps.gov/bost/historyculture/ussconst.htm

Official USS Constitution website:

http://www.history.navy.mil/ussconstitution/index.html

617-242-5670

Handicap access to the ship is via a ramped gangplank to main deck. The deck has 1/2" raised ridges. Navy personnel can assist. The lower decks are down steep staircases.

Restrooms are in the Visitor Center

Public transportation: Green or Orange line to North Station (in Boston proper). Alternative, 93 Bus to Sullivan Station Bunker Hill.

Plan at least an hour to view the Constitution, including a tour.

Web-translate section and narration:
http://www.stevestravelguide.com/?p=1362

Background Information

The Revolutionary War officially ended in 1783 with the Treaty of Paris. In 1785, the United States sold its last remaining naval vessel due to a lack of funds. The same year, two American merchant ships were captured by Algiers.

Eight years later, in 1793, Algiers captured eleven ships and held their crews and cargo for ransom. The new nation was undergoing one of its first tests.

Waking up to the need to protect its interests, Congress authorized the Naval Act of 1794. This act allocated the funds to build six frigates that were to become the start of the US Navy. Four of the frigates were designed to carry forty-four guns, and two were to carry thirty-six guns.

The USS Constitution, begun in November 1794 was the third of the six original frigates. She was built, starting in November 1794, across the river from its current berth, at the Boston shipyard of Edmund Hartt.

The Constitution's design took into account the reality that the United States could not match the European states navies' heavy "ships of the line." The much smaller US Navy needed to be strong enough to defeat other frigates, yet fast enough to avoid fights with heavier ships.

Her design was unusual for the time in that she was very long and narrow, and mounted heavy guns. She also had a diagonal rib scheme for extra strength. The primary materials were pine and oak, including southern live oak from Georgia. Live oak is extremely dense, heavy and hard, and is the reason that the Constitution could survive heavy cannon shots without damage. This unique design was to be proven many times in battle.

Originally designed for forty-four guns, the Constitution was often equipped with fifty or more. During the War of 1812, she carried thirty 24-pound cannons on the gun deck (one level down from the upper deck), twenty-two 32-pound carronades (shorter range cannon) on the upper deck and two chase guns each at the bow and stern.

Peace with Algiers was announced in 1796, and construction was halted before any of the ships could be launched. Prompted by President George Washington, Congress agreed to continue funding the three ships closest to completion – the USS United States, Constellation, and the Constitution. The Constitution finally slipped into the waters of Boston harbor in October 1797.

The Constitution served briefly during the Quasi-War with France from 1798-1800. During this conflict, she served three tours of duty in the West

Indies and participated in several actions. She returned to Boston in 1801 where she was put into reserve. Prior to her next duty service, her bottom was resheathed with copper from Paul Revere's factory – the first copper rolling mill in the United States.

In 1803, under Captain Edward Commodore Preble, she sailed to Africa's northern coast to confront Barbary ships during the First Barbary War. There she participated in multiple actions, the most significant being the Battle of Tripoli Harbor. She was on station during this conflict for over four years, not returning to Boston until 1807.

The Constitution's most famous actions took place during the War of 1812. In August, about 700 miles east of Boston, the Constitution met the British frigate, the HMS Guerriere. Within about 35 minutes, the Guerriere was a wreck and too damaged to be salvaged. After transferring the wounded and prisoners to the Constitution, the Guerriere was set afire and blown up.

It was in this fight that the Constitution earned the nickname of "Old Ironsides." When many of the Guerriere's shots were observed to bounce harmlessly off her hull, an American sailor reportedly exclaimed "Hussah, her sides are made of iron."

On December 29 of that year, the Constitution fought and defeated the HMS Java off the coast of Brazil. The Java was defeated in about two hours. As with the HMS Guerriere, she was too damaged to be captured had to be destroyed at sea.

The Constitution participated in several other actions, including the defeat of the HMS Pictou, and the capture of HMS Cyane and HMS Levant. The Levant was later recaptured by the British. The Constitution also had two cat-and-mouse escapes from superior British squadrons. She additionally captured a number of British merchant vessels.

After the War of 1812, the USS Constitution served in the Mediterranean squadron. This service was mostly uneventful, but there were notable discipline issues regarding the behavior of the crew while in port.

The normal service life for a ship during this period was ten to fifteen years. When the Constitution was thirty-one, a service order was put in to request money for repairs. Catching wind of the request, a Boston newspaper erroneously reported that she was about to be scrapped. Within two days, Oliver Wendell Holmes' poem "Old Ironsides" was published. The ensuing public outcry incited efforts to save her, and the refurbishment costs were approved. The USS Constitution made the first use of Dry Dock 1.

Most of the Constitution's subsequent duties were ceremonial. She ferried ambassadors ministers to new posts and performed various patrolling duties in the Mediterranean, South America, Africa and Asia. Just prior to the Civil War, she became a training ship.

There were attempts to make her seaworthy once again to attend the Paris Exposition of 1878, but these were unsuccessful. In 1881, she was deemed unfit for service. The Constitution was finally returned to the

Charlestown Navy Yard in 1897.

In the early 1900's, there were several attempts to refurbish her, but all failed. In 1905, the Secretary of the Navy suggested that she be towed out to sea and used as target practice. Public outcry prompted Congress to authorize $100,000 for her restoration. By 1907 she began to serve as a museum ship with tours offered to the public.

Since that time she has undergone multiple refurbishments and cruises, including a three-year, 90-port tour of the nation that started in 1931 and transited the Panama Canal in 1932. Her most extensive refurbishment was from 1992 to 1995. She sailed under her own power in 1997, in honor of her 200th birthday.

The Constitution typically makes one "turnaround cruise" each year during which she is towed out into Boston Harbor to perform demonstrations, including a gun drill. She is then returned to her dock, where she is berthed in the opposite direction to ensure that she weathers evenly. Attendance on the turnaround cruse is based on a lottery draw and is a highly prized ticket.

USS Constitution's Gun Deck

Charlestown Navy Yard

US Naval Facility Since 1800

The Charlestown Navy Yard is home to the USS Constitution, the USS Cassin Young, one of the first two dry docks in the US, and the USS Constitution Museum.

Great fun. Plan for a several hour visit.

The Museum is free, donation requested

Open 9-5 daily. Closed Christmas, New Year's Day and Thanksgiving

National Park Service website:

http://www.nps.gov/bost/historyculture/cny.htm

Official Charlestown Navy Yard website:

http://www.charlestownonline.net/navyyard.htm

National Park Service Maritime History website:

http://www.nps.gov/nr/travel/maritime/bns.htm

USS Constitution Museum website:

http://www.ussconstitutionmuseum.org/

Museum phone: (617) 426-1812

Public transportation: Green or Orange line to North Station (in Boston proper). Alternative, 93 Bus to Sullivan Station Bunker Hill.

Plan at least an hour for a cursory view of the Navy Yard. If visiting the Navy Yard along with Constitution, plan 2+ hours.

If coming from downtown, the Water Shuttle from Long Wharf is an excellent and fun way to travel and see the harbor at the same time.

Web-translate section and narration:
http://www.stevestravelguide.com/?p=1375

Background Information

In 1800, the government purchased the land for the Charlestown Navy Yard at Moulton's Point, and established the yard itself shortly thereafter. (Moulton's Point is where the British troops landed for their attack on the Patriots during the Battle of Bunker Hill.) In 1814, the yard launched the first US ship of the line, the USS Independence.

Rigging on the USS Constitution

Multiple Navy Yard ships saw service in the Civil War - however, it was primarily a repair and storage facility until the 1890s. At that time, it started to build steel-hulled ships.

The Navy Yard reached its height of activity during World War II, with peak employment in 1943 of 50,128 men and women - working around the clock, 7 days a week. The yard then covered 130 acres with 86 buildings and 3.5 million square feet of floor space. A second dry dock was also added.

During this peak period, the Navy Yard could build a Destroyer Escort in four months and an LST (Landing Ship Tank) in less than four weeks. Overall, between 1939 and 1945, the Navy Yard built 30 destroyers, 60 escort vessels, overhauled and repaired 3,500 ships, and outfitted over 11,000.

After World War II, the Navy Yard was involved with upgrading the fleet and modifying World War II ships for Cold War service. Being so far from the fighting, the Navy Yard did not receive much work during the Korean and Vietnam conflicts.

As part of cost cutting measures, President Nixon ordered the yard closed in 1974. Many Bostonians believe the Nixon administration made that decision to punish Massachusetts, the only state to vote against him in 1972.

Since the closing, the bulk of the facility has been recycled and developed. The thirty acres that were transferred to the National Park Service became part of the Boston National Historical Park, with a mission "to interpret the art and history of naval shipbuilding."

Dry Dock 1

Dry Dock 1 & USS Cassin Young

Dry Dock 1 was one of the first two dry docks put into service the United States, missing out on the honor of being first by only a week - that distinction when to Norfolk, Virginia. Dry docks are important to avoid the tedious, expensive and dangerous process of careening or "heaving down" a ship to work on its hull. Careening requires leaning a ship over on its side, which puts great stress on its hull and only exposes one side at a time. In fact, sometimes ships would sink during the careening process.

The need for dry docks was understood from the beginning of the US Navy, but construction did not begin until 1827 and then took six years to complete. The project was designed and under the control of Loammi Baldwin, considered the father of civil engineering in the United States.

The granite for this project, as well as the dry dock in Norfolk, came from Quincy – the same site that provided the granite used for the Bunker Hill Monument. Dry Dock 1 opened in June of 1833 and its first customer was the USS Constitution.

There are excellent interpretive displays that show how the dry dock works and illustrates the alternative careening method.

USS Cassin Young

The USS Cassin Young is a World War II Fletcher-Class Destroyer commissioned on the last day of 1943. She served with distinction in the Pacific, including during the Battle of Leyte Gulf. She received damage during two separate kamikaze attacks during 1945, one of which killed twenty-two and wounded forty-five sailors.

Visitors can tour the ship, but check

8-Sided Muster House

as the ship is scheduled for refurbishment. ID is required.

Muster House

The interesting eight-sided Muster House was built in 1852 and was an administrative building for the Navy Yard. The clock and bell were used to assemble civilian employees for work at a time when most workers did not wear watches.

Rope Walk

Rope has always been is an essential element of ships, so having quality and production control was a key aspect of the US Navy's strategic plan. The USS Constitution, for example, requires over four miles of rope.

The Ropewalk at the Navy Yard produced most of the cordage used by US Navy between 1838 and 1955 - in 1942 alone producing over 4 million pounds! It had a ¼ mile of rope-laying area, allowing it to produce rope of up to 1200 feet in length as rope is twisted in a straight line. Its innovative steam-powered machinery could produce rope of much higher strength than manual techniques. The Ropewalk was used until 1971.

Although the building is still standing, it is boarded up and there is not much to see. There are interpretive displays in the National Park Service Visitor Center that you walk through prior to boarding the USS Constitution. These explain the rope making process and illustrate the rope walk in operation.

Commandant's House

The Commandant's House was built in 1805 and was home to the Navy Yard's commanders and their families for many years. It has hosted five U.S. presidents and many dignitaries and foreign heads of state. There are no visitors allowed inside.

Stop 16 – Bunker Hill Monument

"The Whites of Their Eyes"

The monument is located on Breed's Hill at the site of the Patriot redoubt during the Battle of Bunker Hill, which was fought on June 17, 1775.

Free

Daily 9 - 5; last climb at 4:30. July and August 9 - 6; last climb at 5:30

Official website:

http://www.nps.gov/bost/historyculture/bhm.htm

617-242-5641

Handicap access to the lodge next to monument is via a ramp. The monument has 294 steps to the top.

Restrooms are in Bunker Hill Museum basement, across the street.

The Bunker Hill Museum (recommended - across the street), is fully accessible with elevators and restrooms.

Museum website:

http://www.nps.gov/bost/historyculture/bhmuseum.htm

Web-translate section and narration:

http://www.stevestravelguide.com/?p=1370

Background information

Most visitors to the Bunker Hill Monument will stop at the Bunker Hill Museum, and we highly recommend visiting. Run by the National Park Service, the museum is just across the street from the steps to the base of the monument. It is excellent, featuring very well done interpretive displays and dioramas and occasional programs, which are often oriented to children. There are full bathroom facilities and it is handicap accessible. Everything is free.

Proceeding across the street from the museum and up the steps to the monument, you will pass the statue of Colonel William Prescott (pictured above the chapter heading), Patriot commander during the battle. Some legends identify Prescott as the man who uttered "don't fire until you see the whites of their eyes." Two superior officers were present at the battle, Major Generals Israel Putnam and Joseph Warren, but both declined to take command from Prescott.

The current obelisk is the second monument erected to commemorate the battle. The first was an 18-foot wooden pillar with a gilt urn that was erected in 1794. In 1823, the Bunker Hill Monument Association was formed by a group of prominent citizens who desired a more fitting memorial.

The 221-foot high monument is located on Breed's Hill, at the site of the Patriot redoubt during the battle. The monument is constructed of granite from Quincy, Massachusetts - the same site that provided the granite for Dry Dock 1 in the Charlestown Navy Yard. A special railroad, the first common carrier in the United States, was built to haul the granite from Quincy to Boston. The final leg of the granite's journey across the harbor was by barge.

Construction started in 1827 but was not completed until 1843 as there were many funding-related delays. To finish the project, the Monument Association actually had to sell off part of their original land, leaving only the summit of Breed's Hill that you see today.

The small exhibit lodge adjacent to the monument was constructed in the late 1800s and houses a few statues and paintings, including a particularly good one of Doctor/General Joseph Warren. The Bunker Hill Monument Association maintained the monument and grounds until 1919 when it was turned over to the Commonwealth of Massachusetts. In 1976 the monument was transferred to the National Park Service.

To ascend the 294 steps to the top of the monument, pass through the lodge and head up. It is recommended that you be confident in your ability to complete the round trip as there is no elevator and no place to sit down, except on the staircase. Climbers to the top will enjoy a great view of Boston and the surrounding areas.

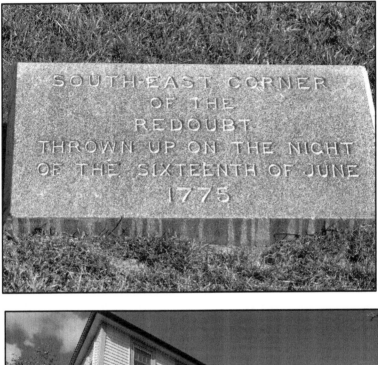

Patriot Redoubt by Bunker Hill & nearby Warren Tavern (1780)

Side Trips: Cambridge, Lexington, Concord, Adams NHP, & Boston Harbor Islands

Web-translate sections:
http://www.stevestravelguide.com/?p=1677
http://www.stevestravelguide.com/?p=1699

Cambridge & Harvard Square

Cambridge, capitalized as "Newe Town" in 1632, is about five miles up the Charles River from Boston. It was established soon after Boston's Puritan settlers arrived to provide a safe haven in event of an attack on the coastal Boston. The original village was located at the first convenient river crossing west of Boston, at what is now Harvard Square. Harvard College was founded here in 1636. The town served as the headquarters for the Patriot troops during the Siege of Boston.

Most tourists will want to visit Harvard University and take in the Revolutionary sites around Harvard Square. The best way to visit the area in a few hours is via a walking tour, which is offered by several companies.

I can recommend the tours from Cambridge Historical Tours, website at http://cambridgehistoricaltours.org/ phone 617.520.4030. There are excellent free Student-Led & Self-Guided Walking Tours of Harvard Yard available directly from Harvard: http://www.harvard.edu/visitors/audio-tours. For information about the free student-led tours visit: http://www.harvard.edu/visitors/tours.

The Longfellow House, run by the National Park Service, is on Tory Row and only a short walk from Harvard Square. In addition to being the home of poet Henry Wadsworth Longfellow, it was George Washington's headquarters during the Siege of Boston. The NPS offers seasonal ranger-led tours, talks, and neighborhood walks. For hours and tour times, visit the website at *http://www.nps.gov/long* or call 617-876-4491. Admission is free.

Public transportation from Boston to Harvard Square is easy and quick via the MBTA service to the Harvard Square station.

Lexington & Concord

The nearby colonial towns of Lexington and Concord were the sites of the first significant battle of the American Revolution. A visit is worthwhile and an easy 1/2 to full day trip from Boston. Each year Massachusetts celebrates Patriots Day, around the April 19th anniversary of the battle, with reenactments and parades. (My YouTube Channel has an introductory video – see Links & References.)

Most of the Lexington sites center on the Lexington Battle Green, at the site of the first skirmish. For maps and information, start at the Visitor Center, located next to the Battle Green. For Lexington information, go to http://www.lexingtonchamber.org or call 781-862-1450. There is a downloadable self-guided walking tour of the Battle Green area along with other information from the Lexington Historical Society website at www.lexingtonhistory.org.. The Tourism Committee runs free tours given by costumed guides, spring through fall seasons. The narrated Liberty Ride, which runs to all the major sites from Lexington to Concord is a great way to travel and learn history at the same time – see below for information.

Important visitor sites close to the Battle Green include the Minuteman Statue (paradoxically, Lexington never had minutemen, only militia), the Buckman Tavern (where the Minutemen gathered just prior to the battle), the Hancock-Clarke House (where Samuel Adams and John Hancock stayed the night before the battle), and the Old Belfry. The Historical Society runs the Hancock-Clark House, Buckman Tavern, and Munroe Tavern. All offer tours by excellent docents, and each offers a unique perspective.

The Munroe Tavern is about a mile east of the town center. It was the site of the British headquarters and field hospital during their retreat back to Boston. A packaged ticket for admission to the Munroe Tavern, the Hancock-Clarke House and the Buckman Tavern is available at any of the three houses: $12 for adults and $8 for children 6-16. Individual house admissions are $7 and $5 respectively. Contact the Lexington Historical Society to confirm the operating hours, which vary by season.

Concord was the site of the battle at North Bridge, but it has a lot more to offer if you have time. For visitor information in the town center, go to the Concord Chamber of Commerce; open from the end of March until late October, and on the Thanksgiving weekend. Walking tours are available; admission is charged. The Chamber can be reached at 978-369-3120; or access their website at http://concordchamberofcommerce.org. There is a downloadable Concord Walking Map on the website.

Important non-Revolutionary Concord sites include the Orchard House (home of Louisa May Alcott, where she wrote "Little Women;" admission charge), the Concord Museum (which has one of the two lanterns hung at Old North Church; admission charge), and The Wayside (home to the Alcotts, Nathaniel Hawthorne and Margaret Sidney; admission charge).

Most Revolutionary-centric visitors head directly to the Minuteman National Historical Park to visit the area around North Bridge. It is about 1/2 mile from the town center. For more on the Minuteman Park, see below.

For public transportation from Boston to Lexington, take the MBTA Red line to Alewife station and connect with either the #76 or #62 buses to Lexington. The ride from Alewife to Lexington is about 25 minutes.

To Concord center, take the MBTA Commuter Rail from Boston's North Station. The Fitchburg Line train stops at the Concord Depot on Thoreau Street. From the Depot, the North Bridge is a 1.5-mile walk.

For visitors to both Lexington and Concord traveling without cars, the best option is to travel to Lexington and take the Liberty Ride trolley. The trolley stops near all major sites in both towns and provides hop-on and off service, giving the opportunity to hike portions of the Battle Road. It runs on weekends in April and May, then daily until October 28. Adult tickets are $25, children 5-17 are $10. It also includes admission to the Lexington houses mentioned above. For Liberty Ride information, call 781 781-862-0500, website at http://www.libertyride.us/libertyride.html.

Minuteman National Historical Park

The Minuteman National Historical Park, run by the National Park Service, has two sections. The eastern section follows the Battle Road from just outside Lexington into Concord. The western section covers the area around North Bridge, just beyond Concord center. Both have visitor centers and ranger-guided tours and talks. All programs are free, with the exception of an admission charge to the Wayside (now closed for renovation – check); $5 for adults, free for children 16 and under. For full park information visit the park's website at http://www.nps.gov/mima or call 978-369-6993.

The visitor center at the eastern end of the park

North Bridge seen from the Park Service visitor center

(nearest Lexington) features a very good multi-media show, "The Road to Revolution," especially entertaining for children. The center also has exhibits, dioramas, and other battle-related information. Rangers are on duty to answer questions and there is a small gift shop.

The five mile Battle Road makes for a great hike and much of it has been restored to a state similar to Revolutionary times. Be sure to visit the Hartwell Tavern, which is representative of an authentic period home-tavern and has ranger-programs from May through October. The Paul Revere Capture Site, just off Route 2A, is a frequent visitor stop.

West of Battle Road, and the closest stop to Concord center, is The Wayside. In Revolutionary times, The Wayside was home to the muster master of the Concord Minute Men. Later, it became the "Home of Authors," with its residents including Louisa May Alcott, Nathaniel Hawthorne, and Harriett Lothrop (Margaret Sidney). The Wayside is next door to Orchard House, which charges a separate admission fee and is not associated with the Park.

The western section around North Bridge has a small visitor center set spectacularly on the hill overlooking the bridge. It features a few small exhibits and a very good three dimensional map that illustrates the topography of the important battle sites. It is located in a mansion that once belonged to the Buttrick family. Major John Buttrick was the Patriot who ordered the colonials to fire on the British at North Bridge.

For public transportation to the eastern visitor center from Boston, take the MBTA Red line to Alewife station and connect with the #76 bus to the Old Mass Ave & Marrett Road stop in Lexington. Ask the driver to point out the stop. There is no service on Sunday. To the western section, follow the directions to Concord center, above. The Liberty Ride stops at both sections as well as at Hartwell Tavern, Meriam's Corner, North Bridge and other park sites.

Adams National Historical Park

John Adam's Birthplace (c. 1681)

An easy, rewarding, and often-overlooked Freedom Trail side-trip is to the Adams National Historical Park in Quincy. The park includes the homes of American presidents John Adams (the famous Patriot and 2nd US President), his son, John Quincy Adams (the 6th president), and their descendants from 1720 to 1927. The park is right off of the MBTA Red line and is a simple, quick, and inexpensive trip from Boston. The park is open from mid-April until mid-November. Check their webs--ite at http://www.nps.gov/adam or call 617-770-1175.

A visit starts at the NPS visitor center - access to the homes is only permitted via ranger-led tours. Tours run two hours and cost $5 for adults; children under 16 and holders of a National Park *America the Beautiful* Passes are free. Before leaving the visitor center, view the excellent short film, "Enduring Legacy," that overviews the Adams' lives and accomplishments – it is excellent.

The first stop is at the presidents' birthplaces. To start, you will visit the wonderful, sparse, "saltbox" house (c. 1681) where John was born in 1735. Only 75 feet away is the house where John and Abigail gave birth to John Quincy in 1767. That house also holds the law office where John drafted the Massachusetts Constitution, which later served as the model for the US Constitution.

The next stop is at the "Old House." Built in 1731, it was purchased by John and Abigail as a more suitable residence after their return from John's diplomatic posting to London in 1788. The Adams family expanded the home from its original seven rooms to what you visit today. It was also home to John Quincy, his son Charles Francis (ambassador to Great Britain during the Civil War) and their descendants. It served as a summer White House and is full of original family artifacts and art that helps tell the Adams' story - a real treasure to visit.

Next door to the Old House, set in a beautiful garden, is the Stone Library, built in 1873. This serves as the John Quincy Adams presidential library and holds over 14,000 books, artifacts and family paintings.

Across the street from the visitor center, but not part of the National Park, is the United First Parish Church. The Church contains the tombs of John, Abigail, John Quincy and Louisa Catherine Adams, website at http://www.ufpc.org/. Founded in 1636 as a branch of the Puritan church in Boston, this is the fourth Church building erected on this site. Designed by Alexander

Crypt of John and Abigail Adams

Paris (also designer of Quincy Market), it was completed in 1828, with granite and funding from John Adams. If you have time, take the brief tour of the church and the crypt; a small donation is requested. Tours are available on the same schedule as the National Historical Park, from mid-April through mid-November.

Boston Harbor Islands

View of Boston from Georges Island Artillery Platform

A fantastic trip and relaxing change from Revolutionary Boston is a visit to the Harbor Islands National Recreation Area. At the Islands you can visit a Civil War era fort, swim, picnic, hike, bird watch, camp, enjoy a concert, or just delight on the wonderful, narrated cruise through the Harbor. For the younger visitors there is even a playground with an amazing view of the Boston skyline. The Islands are a cooperative effort between the National Park Service and various Commonwealth, City and private groups.

The park itself features 12 islands and peninsulas, and even the oldest active lighthouse station in the United States (used since 1716, only accessible via a special "Lighthouse Tour"); practically, you can visit a maximum of two Islands per day - visiting a single Island requires at least ½ day, but don't rush. There is a snack shack with a seafood menu on Georges Island, but the food quality can be variable – so you may want to pack a lunch. There is an expertly-staffed pavilion on the Rose Kennedy Greenway between Quincy Market and Long Wharf to help plan your visit, purchase ferry tickets, etc.

Although ferries run from several suburban locations, most visitors will take the ferry the north side of Long Wharf (by Christopher Columbus Park); the ferries take you to either George's or Spectacle Island. From George's Island, during the summer, there are connections to other islands. Fares are: Adults, $15; children 4-11, $9; over 65, $11, inter-island, $3. Regular service runs May through Columbus Day in the fall, but there are various winter visit opportunities. Definitely visit the website for current and detailed visiting and transportation information.

There is a very well done Visitor Center on Georges Island with interpretive exhibits highlighting the Islands' history, their role in the defense of Boston, the impacts of changing military technology, even the respective diets of enlisted men and officers – fascinating even for the non-military-oriented visitor. Unless you know you want your stop to be Spectacle Island, stop here first, watch the eight minute video and plan the rest of your visit. Rangers are there to help.

There are excellent Ranger-led tours of the Civil War era Fort Warren, which was built between 1833 and 1861 (self-guided tours are also available). During the Civil War, the fort served as a prison for over 1,000 Confederate personnel, the most famous the Confederate Vice President Alexander Stephens. Fort Warren remained active through the Spanish-American War and World War I. During World War II, it was part of the harbor's defense from German U-boats. Over the years it was modified to accommodate changing cannon technology. It was permanently decommissioned in the 1950's when guided missiles obsoleted cannon for coastal defense.

A visit is highly recommended and suitable for all ages. Handicap access, however, is limited; please check the website for detailed information.

Useful links for a Boston Harbor Islands visit:

- The official website: http://www.bostonharborislands.org/
- National Park Service website: http://www.nps.gov/boha/parkmgmt/index.htm
- National Park Service map of the Islands http://www.nps.gov/hfc/carto/PDF/BOHAmap1.pdf
- Boston Harbor Islands YouTube channel: http://www.youtube.com/user/Bostonharborislands
- Ferry website: http://bostonsbestcruises.com/boston-harbor-islands-schedules-and-fares
- The Boston Harbor Island Alliance website: http://www.islandalliance.org/

Excellent Visitor Center on Georges Island

Time Line

Below is a chronological list of important events that relate to Boston history and the places you will visit on the Freedom Trail. Other important events are provided for context - each of these is noted with an (H). Where there is important information about the event or place elsewhere in the Guide, hyperlinks are provided.

1492 - (H) Columbus "discovers" America.
1530 – (H) Henry VIII drives the English Reformation, breaking the Church of England with the Catholic Church.
1565 - (H) First permanent European settlement (Spanish) in continental America at St. Augustine, Florida.
1607 - (H) Jamestown colony founded on the Chesapeake Bay.
1608 - (H) Quebec City founded.
1614 - (H) English explorer, Captain John Smith, while mapping New England coast from Penobscot (Maine) to Cape Cod (Massachusetts), notes Shawmut Peninsula (Boston); (H) New Amsterdam founded by the Dutch on the tip of Manhattan Island (New York City).
1620 - Pilgrim separatists leave and found Plymouth.
1629 - Royal charter granted to Massachusetts Bay Colony; Charlestown MA founded.
1630 - Led by John Winthrop, Puritans leave for America. The group founds Boston.
1631 - King's Chapel Burying Ground founded.
1634 - Boston Common purchased from William Blaxton.
1635 - Boston Latin School founded.
1636 - Harvard College founded.
1640 - Boston population 1,200.
1650 - Boston population 2,000.
1651 - The first Navigation Act is passed.
1660 - Granary Burying Ground and Copp's Hill Burying Ground are founded; Boston population 3,000.
1682 - (H) Philadelphia founded.
1664 - (H) New Amsterdam turned over to the British - renamed New York.
1684 - King James II revokes the Massachusetts Bay Colony's unique charter; Sir Edmund Andros is installed as governor in 1686.
1688 - King's Chapel founded.
1689 - Governor Andros is forced to resign. (H) William and Mary's reign starts.
1680 - Paul Revere House constructed.
1690 - Boston population 7,000.
1691 - Massachusetts gets a new Charter.
1710 - Boston population 9,000.
1711 - Old State House and the Old Corner Book Store are built after the Great Fire of 1711.

1714 - Union Oyster House building constructed.

1720 - Boston population 12,000.

1723 - Christ Church (Old North Church) built.

1729 - Old South Meeting House built.

1730 - Boston population 13,000.

1733 - Molasses Act enacted.

1742 - Faneuil Hall built; Boston population 16,382.

1750 - King's Chapel built.

1759 - French and Indian War (Seven Years War) is over (treaty not signed until 1763); British treasury is drained.

1760 - Ebenezer Hancock House built; King George III takes the British throne; Writs of Assistance enacted; Boston population 16,000.

1761 - James Otis argues against Writs of Assistance in the Old State House.

1765 - Stamp Act is enacted, resulting in riots in Boston and other cities.

1766 - Stamp Act is repealed.

1767 - Townshend Acts passed; non-importation boycott.

1768 - Circular Letter; protestors riot in Boston; British troops land to maintain order.

1770 - Boston Massacre takes place.

1772 - Committees of Correspondence formed.

1773 - Tea Act passed; Boston Tea Party.

1774 - "Intolerable Acts" passed; port of Boston closed; General Gage appointed governor; Minute Men formed; (H) First Continental Congress meets in Philadelphia.

1775 - Paul Revere's Ride; Battles of Lexington and Concord; (H) Second Continental Congress meets in Philadelphia; Battle of Bunker Hill; Siege of Boston starts; George Washington arrives to take command.

1776 - Dorchester Heights fortified; Siege of Boston lifted as British leave Boston; (H) Declaration of Independence signed.

1781 - (H) Battle of Yorktown, British surrender ending American Revolution (peace treaty signed in 1783).

1797 - USS Constitution constructed.

1798 - Massachusetts State House opens, designed by Charles Bulfinch.

1800 - Charlestown Navy Yard established; Boston population 24,937.

1803 - Faneuil Hall rebuilt by Charles Bullfinch.

1804 - St. Stephens Church on Hanover Street built.

1809 - Park Street Church built.

1810 - Boston population 33,787.

1812 - War starts with Great Britain; USS Constitution defeats British frigate HMS Guerriere.

1820 - Boston population 43,298.

1825-6 - Quincy Market built.

1825-1843 - Bunker Hill Monument built.

1862 - Old City Hall built.

1863 - The MA 54th attacks Fort Wagner in South Carolina.

Background & History

Boston Topography

To web-translate Boston Topography through Puritan Inspired Democratic Government (password protected): http://www.stevestravelguide.com/?p=1296

The Boston you visit today is very different from the Boston of the sixteenth and seventeenth centuries. Its topography was to play a key role in influencing the events of the Revolutionary period.

When the first visitors arrived, they found a salamander-shaped, rocky, hilly, peninsula that was formed by erosion at the end of the last ice age. It was small, only two miles long and a mile wide at its largest point. It was called Shawmut by the Native Americans, but none still lived there when the white settlers arrived.

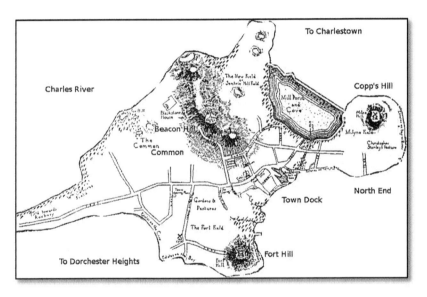

Annotated Extract from Map of Boston Before 1645

The peninsula was dominated by three hills, hence its early name of Trimountaine or Trimountain, which was later shortened to Tremont. There was Copp's Hill (in the North End), Beacon Hill (which had three summits at the time), and Fort Hill (in today's financial district).

Shawmut was joined to the mainland by a low-lying, narrow, windswept isthmus - later called Boston Neck. The neck often flooded at high tide and was impassable during stormy weather, making the peninsula effectively an island.

The original peninsula was only half the size of the existing land form.

The rest was created by land reclamation projects, which started in a small way soon after the Puritans arrived in 1630 (you can see the 1630 water line marked in the pavement near the Samuel Adams Statue behind Faneuil Hall).

The primary landfill projects took place between 1807 and about 1900, although some reclamation projects extended until almost 2000. Much of the land for the earlier projects came from the leveling of Fort Hill and from Beacon Hill, which had two of its three peaks razed and the remaining one (the current Beacon Hill) reduced to about half its original size. The largest project, the filling in of the Back Bay, ran between 1856 and about 1894. For that project, gravel was transported in on a specially built train line from Needham, about twenty miles away. One of the first steam shovels was used to fill the gravel cars for the trains, which ran around the clock for almost fifty years.

The picture below displays an annotated version of a map of Boston in 1895. The black tracing illustrates Boston's landform in 1775. The primary landfill projects along with their rough timeframes are described. The major landmark neighborhoods of the Back Back, Beacon Hill, the North End, the South End, Copley Square and the Fenway are identified.

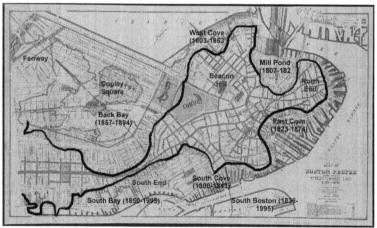

Outline of Boston in 1775 showing Major Landfill Projects

To the west of Boston Neck were the mudflats and salt marshes of the Back Bay, an estuary of the Charles River. To the east was the water of Boston Harbor. There were two major coves - one to the north that was quickly dammed to create Mill Cove, and one to the south on the harbor (Town Cove) that was to serve as the site of the town dock. The northern part of the peninsula (the North End) was connected to the main portions of the peninsula by a small neck of land.

The peninsula was surrounded on three sides by land masses. To the north across the Charles River was Charlestown (also a peninsula) and Chelsea. To the west, connected via Boston Neck, was the major link to the mainland landmass. The first town past the Neck was called Roxbury. To the south was imposing Dorchester Heights, which overlooked the harbor. Soon after its founding, Boston established ferries serving Charlestown and Chelsea.

Boston's primary access to the outside world was its harbor, as the single road to Roxbury was frequently impassable. People, produce and even firewood moved into the city primarily via the harbor.

Boston's economy was highly dependent on trade and access to the sea. Shipbuilding and the support of the merchant ecosystem were part and parcel to Boston's economic health.

The closing of the harbor by the British after the Boston Tea Party was devastating - economically and functionally. There was no work, no trade, and not enough to eat. This impacted both Patriot and British/Loyalist populations.

When the Siege of Boston began in mid-1775 after the Battles of Lexington and Concord, the British were bottled into this island, surrounded on three sides, without sufficient troops to break out. When, after receiving reinforcements, they tried to break out, they were effectively parried by the Patriot action at the Battle of Bunker Hill.

Finally, when the Patriots were able to mount cannon on Dorchester Heights and threaten the town and the British fleet in the harbor, the British had to cut their losses and evacuate the city.

Without Boston's unique topography, none of this would have been possible. (It is also fun to realize that much of the land you stand on during a Freedom Trail visit was originally either part of the harbor or the Charles River. This includes Faneuil Hall, Quincy Market, parts of the North End, even part of Boston Common.)

The Reformation

As context for the Puritan's founding of Boston, it is helpful to step back and describe what was happening in Europe that would encourage a major migration to the new world. At the root was the desire for religious freedom.

Throughout Europe during the 15th and 16th centuries, there was growing dissatisfaction with the Catholic Church. There were issues with its doctrine, its ritualistic nature, and the hierarchical way in which it was governed. This was compounded by the buying and selling of influential church positions and outright corruption. All this led to an attempt to reform the Catholic Church - the "Reformation."

The Reformation's official starting point is considered to be October 1517, when Martin Luther posted his "Ninety-Five Theses" on a church in Wittenberg, Saxony (now Germany). There were many different views on the best new doctrine to follow, and over time, the different views evolved into various Protestant denominations. These included Lutheran, Baptist, Anglican (the Church of England), and the Congregationalists (the Puritans).

[Protestantism differed from Catholicism in several key ways. First is the belief in "scripture alone" - that the Bible is the only and infallible source of authority for the church. Second is the belief in "justification in faith alone" - that salvation is achieved solely through faith, independent of whatever else a person has done during their life. The third is the "universal priesthood of believers". This implies the right and duty of the Christian laity not only to read the Bible in their native language, but also to take part in the governing and all the public affairs of the Church.]

Although there was widespread English dissatisfaction with the Catholic Church before, the official English Reformation started in 1530 when King Henry VIII of England, in his quest to produce a male heir, needed to divorce his first queen, Catherine of Aragon. The pope refused to annul the marriage, so Henry had the Church of England break away from the authority of the Pope and the Roman Catholic Church. He then divorced Catherine, but although he was married five more times, was never successful producing a male heir.

[The English state religion and the associated politics was to flip-flop between Catholic and Protestant for the next hundred and fifty years.]

The Church of England, also known as the Anglican Church, was more similar to Catholicism than the other Protestant denominations. It retained many of the trappings, the ceremony, and the hierarchy of the Catholic Church.

When England broke with the Catholic Church, many different Protestant sects vied for power. After Henry's death, his daughter, Queen Elizabeth I (the Virgin Queen, reign 1558-1603), set out to eliminate the "foolish theological quibbling" among the sects. She formalized the Church of England as the official church and instituted Penal Laws to enforce compliance.

Not surprisingly, there was still dissension. Some dissenters joined the Church of England and worked to "purify" the church from within, becoming known as "Puritans." Some refused to join the church, and became known as "Separatists."

King James I (rule 1603-1625) and his successor son, King Charles I (1625-1649) were particularly zealous in enforcing conformity to the Church of England. Those who did not support the Church of England faced persecution and worse. The persecution inflicted on dissenting Protestants, coupled with a poor economy, drove two key groups to leave England in search of religious freedom.

The first group to leave England for the colonies was a relatively poor and agrarian group of Separatists, who became known as the Pilgrims. This group left England for Holland in 1608, and, because they feared losing their identity in Dutch society, departed for America on the Mayflower 1620. They founded the colony of Plymouth (also known as Plimouth or Plimoth), about 40 miles south of Boston.

The second group, made up of Puritans, was more affluent and included educated merchants and businessmen. It was this group that was to found Boston.

Before Europeans & the "Great Dying"

Before white Europeans arrived, New England had been inhabited by Native Americans for over a thousand years. Migrating here after the retreat of the last ice age, by 1500 they had a population likely in excess of 100,000. Originally hunters and gatherers, they had become more agricultural with extensive fields of corn (maize –a major food source), beans squash. By this point the tribes were fundamentally stationary, but shifted dwelling several times year based on weather – winter, autumn hunting, and summer.

The tribes that inhabited New England had a common heritage and belonged to the Algonquian family. They had a fairly common language, and although each tribe had nuances, there was the ability to be understood from Cape Cod to Canada.

At the time of the white man's arrival, there were a number of principle tribes, some warlike and in competition with their neighbors. The names of these tribes have been inherited by many prominent New England towns, rivers and lakes. Among those was the Massachusett (which in the Algonquian language means "people of the great hills"), who were to give their name to the Commonwealth of Massachusetts.

Between 1616 and 1619 a plague wiped out almost ¾ of the New England Native American population, with the devastation worse in the coastal areas where mortality was as high as 95%. The Massachusett saw their population decline from about 3,000 in 1615 to about 500 in 1630, when Boston was founded. A major effect was that when white settlers began arriving, starting in 1620, they encountered very little of the indigenous population. The Native American's ability to resist the Europeans was very weak.

The Coming of the Europeans

As early as the 1500's, it was common that English fishing ships traveled and harvested the areas around Newfoundland. In 1501, the Portuguese explorer Gaspar Corte-Real reached and abducted over 50 Native Americans from what is now the state of Maine; the Native Americans were sold into slavery. In 1523 the Italian Giovanni da Verrazano sailed into Narragansett bay (near present-day Providence, RI) and spent over two weeks trading as a guest of the Natives. After leaving Narragansett, he sailed north and encountered the warlike Abnacki tribe on the coast of Maine.

By the end of the 16th century, European exploration into North America had become common, but was focused on fishing the plentiful herring, haddock and cod. Permanent settlement was non-existent and the fisherman-explorers went home as winter approached. Universally, the Europeans noted that North America was thickly settled with Natives, generally described as handsome and healthy. And, the area seemed ripe for exploitation.

At the end of the 1600s with increasing stability in Elizabethan-era Europe, attention began to shift to capitalization of North American. This resulted in the emergence of trading companies, who desired to set up more permanent settlements to harvest the riches.

English explorer Bartholomew Gosnold, in 1602, established a small post on Cuttyhunk Island (in the Elizabethan Islands near Cape Cod), but had to abandon the outpost as they had insufficient supplies to last the winter. During this visit, Gosnold is also credited with naming "Cape Cod" and discovering Martha's Vineyard. Gosnold voyage succeeding in generating the interest of other explorers. He was later involved in the founding of Jamestown, the first permanent English settlement in North America (1607).

Between 1605-1606, French explorer Samuel de Champlain (known as the founder of "New France" in North America) visited Cape Cod, with plans to establish a French base – this plan was abandoned after skirmishes with the Natives. Champlain participated in the founding of Port-Royal in 1605, the first successful French Settlement in North America. In 1608, Champlain founded what is now Quebec City, on the Saint Lawrence river in Canada.

Englishman Sir Ferdinando Gorges (known as the "Father of English Colonization in North America"), had interest in creating settlements settling in Maine – which at the time was considered "the Northern Parte of Virginia,". In 1605, he was part of the sponsoring group for an expedition under Captain George Waymouth. Waymouth was sent to explore the area of New England. During his voyage, Waymouth captured five Native Americans who he brought back to England. According to some accounts, one of the captured Indians was Squanto, who was to play a key role in helping the Pilgrims survive their first winter in North America. After 1605, many voyages carried one or more as guides and interpreters.

In 1607, again initiated by by Sir Fernando Gorges, the Sagadahoc settlement (also known as the Popham settlement) at the base of Kennebec near modern Portland, Maine (1606-7) was the first English attempt at colonizing New England. However, it was abandoned after only one year, probably more due to changes in leadership than lack of success.

In 1614, the English explorer Captain John Smith was ordered by the future King Charles I, to set sail to America to assess commercial opportunities. Smith reached land in present-day Maine and made his way south to Cape Cod, making contact with natives and mapping out the coastline. Smith called the region "New England." During the mapping,

Smith noted the land that was to become Boston.

The Pilgrims & Early Settlements

The first group to leave England and establish a permanent settlement was a relatively poor and agrarian group of about 100 Separatists, who became known as the Pilgrims. This group left England for Holland in 1608, and, because they feared losing their identity in Dutch society, departed for America on the *Mayflower* in 1620. They founded the colony of Plymouth (also known as Plimouth or Plimoth), about 40 miles south of Boston.

The Plymouth settlers had to confront many difficulties during their first winter including the risk of starvation and the lack of appropriate housing. By the end of the winter of 1620-21, nearly half of the original passengers had died.

In the spring of 1621, the Pilgrims met and received assistance from Native Americans from the Patuxet tribe (a small tribe subservient to the Wampanoag). Notably, they received assistance from a Native American named Squanto (Tisquantum in the native language), who had learned English while in Europe.

The assistance of Indians was vital. They taught the colonists how to farm corn, where and how to catch fish, how to make items and even assisted in setting up trading posts for furs. After a successful 1621 harvest, the Pilgrims gathered with Squanto, the chief of the Wampanoags, Massassoit, and approximately 90 other Native Americans, and celebrated the first Thanksgiving.

There were several other failed settlements, notably the one at Wessagusset, the site of present day Weymouth, about sixteen miles south of downtown Boston. The first colony (1622-23) was under provisioned and unsuccessful. A second colony, later in 1623, named Weymouth, was also unsuccessful but some of the colonists remained and others migrated to the present day Boston area.

The first permanent European settler in Boston proper was likely a migrant from the Wessagusset colony, Samuel Maverick. Maverick settled first in the Chelsea area in 1624, then moved to Noddles Island in Boston harbor (the site of present day East Boston) and set up a trading post. He may have been one of the first slave owners in Boston as he purchased several natives from the Tortugas in 1638.

The first white settler of the Shawmut peninsula (Shawmut is the Massachusett word for "place of clear waters"), Boston proper was William Blaxton (Blackstone), a reclusive hermit. He had arrived in New England in 1623 as chaplain of the Weymouth colony and when that failed, he migrated to Shawmut and became its first white resident in 1625.

The Dorchester Company & Boston's Founding

In 1623, the Dorchester Company was formed with the intent to profit from the development of fisheries in New England. Fourteen settlers were sent to

Cape Ann, about 40 miles north of Boston. This settlement failed, but a few settlers remained, moving to Naumkeag, the site of present day Salem, Massachusetts.

In 1628, under the leadership of John Endicott, a fishing settlement of the Dorchester Company was established at Naumkeag on Cape Ann. Naumkeag was renamed Salem, the Hebrew word for peace, the following year.

The Dorchester Company failed, but several of its owners reorganized the company as the "New England Company" and were issued a land grant for the territory between the Charles and Merrimac Rivers. The grant was subsequently sold to the "The New England Company for a Plantation in Massachusetts Bay." The New England Company sent about 50 settlers to join the settlers already in Naumkeag.

The New England Company's venture was risky as some of the land identified in their grant was also identified in competing grants. To fix this, they sought a charter from the King that would supersede all prior grants.

King Charles I granted the desired charter to what was now called the "Massachusetts Bay Colony" in 1629. The charter was unique in that it did not stipulate where the annual stockholders' meeting would be held. This simple omission would play a key role in allowing the colony to develop as an independent society with minimal involvement from England.

The Massachusetts Bay Colony was a Puritan company, and the Puritans had suffered significant religious persecution - so much so that they doubted they would be able to accomplish their desired religious reforms in England. The unique provision in the Charter gave them the opportunity to set up their own colony largely free from English persecution and interference. This opportunity was too good to pass up.

In 1629, the Massachusetts Bay Colony's Puritans, under the leadership of John Winthrop, agreed to move the Colony's operations to America. Going forward, all stockholders would need to reside in America, and those who did not want to emigrate agreed to be bought out by those who did. Winthrop carried the charter with him when he came to America in 1630, further isolating it from London's eyes.

This charter allowed The Massachusetts Bay Colony to be the first colony whose board of directors did not reside in England. This also meant that it could be virtually self-governing, reporting only to the Crown. The colony was able to operate this fashion for fifty five years, until the charter was revoked by Charles II in 1684. This was plenty of time for the Puritans' ideals to become entrenched.

Winthrop's Puritan group sailed from England to New England in 1630 with the ambitious mission of creating a new society, a "city upon a hill" (reference from Jesus' Sermon on the Mount), that would be watched by the world. The Puritans' idealized society would balance both civil and ecclesiastical dimensions for the good of the public – all under God's law as is written in the Bible.

The first Puritan group, consisted of 11 ships and about 700 settlers, landed near present day Salem, Massachusetts. They then moved south to Charlestown, where they met settlers who had migrated south from the Naumkeag settlement. Charlestown, however, lacked an adequate water supply.

William Blaxton invited Winthrop and his group to share the water on the Shawmut peninsula. Winthrop and his followers accepted Blaxton's offer and moved to the peninsula, founding "Boston," which they named after a town near their home in Lincolnshire, England.

Winthrop's Puritan group was the first of a wave of Puritan immigration that was to swell to 20,000 by 1640, populating all of New England.

The Puritan Philosophy

The image that many people have of Puritans as a virtuous, ascetic, frugal, hardworking, industrious people who don't have fun is true - but tells only part of the story. (This is the image that many people still hold of people from New England.) The complete picture is far more interesting. The Puritans were a complex blend of religion, business and politics.

The church was at the center of Puritan society, and the brand of Protestantism the Puritans created evolved to what today is called Congregationalism. Congregationalist practice has each congregation as independent, self-funded, and self-governed by its members. The New England "town meeting" form of government grew directly from this practice.

There was no higher authority than the Bible, but Puritans did believe in individualism to the level that allowed for personal interpretation. However, personal freedom was very strongly bounded.

The communal approach to society meant that the community had the right to exercise control over individuals to promote and protect the common interest. Strict enforcement of rules and laws could take place whenever the community was thought to be threatened. In practice, this led to a religious police state where the community had the right to control individuals for the common good.

US President Taft once commented that the Puritans "came to this country to establish freedom of their religion, not the freedom of anybody else's religion."

A citizen had to conform to the Puritan religion and rules, or they were out. Those who did not agree to their rules were prosecuted, often ruthlessly. For example, the Puritans tried to peaceably drive out the Quakers, but when peaceable means failed, whipping and execution quickly followed.

Catholics were treated little better and were universally hated and harangued. Even the Anglicans (they were, after all, pretty close to Catholic) were not able to establish their own church until the Crown started to strongly reassert authority. King's Chapel was established by Royal directive in 1686 - more than 55 years after Boston's founding.

Puritan intolerance and dogmatism was also at the root of the Salem witch trials which resulted in 20 hangings and at least 150 more imprisoned and tortured to confess their sins. Interestingly, in spite of the cinematic images, no witches were burned at the stake. That privilege was reserved for the more brutal days of the European witches, where many tens of thousands were executed.

But all was not bad. In addition to being hard working and industrious, there were many wonderful Puritan traits. There was a strong commitment to education. This was not only so they could read the Bible, but also to help build a society with a robust professional class.

In 1635 the first public school in America, Boston Latin, was founded on the model of the Free Grammar School from the Puritans' home of Boston, in Lincolnshire, England. Boston Latin was to graduate a who's who of American revolutionary thought – including Samuel Adams, Benjamin Franklin, and John Hancock. In 1647 the Puritans passed a law that required elementary schools in all towns of 50 or more families.

In 1636, Harvard College was founded in nearby Cambridge. Harvard was created not only to train students for the ministry, but also for other higher pursuits including law and medicine. Harvard's Revolutionary-era alumni included not only most of the Boston Latin graduates, but also James Otis, Jr., John Adams, and even some prominent Loyalists, such as the English Governor at the time of the Boston Tea Party, Thomas Hutchinson.

Puritans were also charitable, taking care of widows, orphans and the infirm. The less fortunate were taken in and cared for, usually in exchange for work. Of course, there was plenty to and there was no reason for unemployment. Only those unwilling to pitch-in went hungry.

Puritan Inspired Democratic Government

As described above, the Colony of Massachusetts Bay was organized under a unique charter. As with many corporate documents, it had a lot of nuances and intricacies. To begin with, it stated that only freemen (i.e., church members) could become citizens. It also granted the Massachusetts General Court (the legislature) the authority to elect officers and to make laws for the colony.

The General Court's first meeting was held in October of 1630, but was attended by only eight freemen. The eight voted to grant all legislative, executive, and judicial power to a "Council" of the Governor's assistants – which consisted of the eight freemen. The Council set up town boundaries, created taxes, and elected officers. The first Governor elected was John Winthrop.

Anger from the rest of the population over power being confined to this very small Council led to a more inclusive agreement. In that subsequent agreement, the General Court was to be made up of representatives of two delegates elected by each town, along with the Governor's council of advisors, and the Governor. The new General Court was granted authority over taxes as well as other matters.

Coupled with town meetings and Puritan values, Massachusetts developed a highly independent, participative, and representative (at least for church members) form of governing themselves.

Boston's Independent Development

To web-translate Boston's Independent Development through the Boston Massacre (password required):

http://www.stevestravelguide.com/?p=1379

For many years, Boston was simply too small economically to be of much consequence to England. Further, England was very busy with its own internal affairs. This preoccupation included two civil wars in the 1640's, ongoing flip-flopping of the state religion between Anglicanism and Catholicism, a plague in 1665, and the Great Fire of 1666, which burned for five days and destroyed a major part of London. Finally, England formally merged with Scotland to form Great Britain in 1707.

Externally, England was involved in wars with Spain, the Netherlands, and France. Just prior to the American Revolution, these culminated in the first global international conflict - the Seven Years War (known as the French and Indian War in the American theater), which took place between 1756 and 1763.

Triangular Trade and Slaving

The Boston Puritans were an industrious people, and it did not take them long to realize that the fish off of the coast of New England was an excellent product to trade. What evolved became known as "triangular trade," which often involved four points, not three.

In Triangular Trade, a vessel from Boston would be loaded with fish for the West Indies (the Caribbean). The fish would be sold and the vessel loaded with island produce – things like sugar, molasses, tobacco, and salt. These would be sold in Europe – countries that included England, Spain, Portugal and France. From there, the ship would be loaded with European goods to sell in New England. In just a few months, it was possible for a merchant to turn a hefty profit beginning with his cargo of fish.

This trade arrangement also took place in reverse. The fish were shipped to Europe, where they were exchanged for European goods and brandy. From there, they sailed to the west coast of Africa where they traded for gold dust, ivory, mahogany and slaves. This cargo was then sent to the West Indies or to America.

There is documented evidence of Bostonians being involved in slave trade as early as 1638. However, it is not until 1644 that Boston merchants were involved in direct importation of slaves. They were exchanged for sugar in the West Indies, which was then shipped back to Boston to make rum.

Boston slave trading peaked between 1740 and 1769. By then, New England and Boston was the world's leading producer of rum, having 63 distilleries by 1750.

England Tries to Reassert Control

In its first fifty five years of development, the Puritans were able to establish and run their own society. This society, their unique democratic form of government, their fierce independence, morals, and the way they thought played a key role leading up to the American Revolution.

By the time England was coming up for air from their internal affairs, two things had happened. First, Boston had developed into a prosperous, self-governing trade center that was accustomed to managing its own affairs. Second, and initially of greater importance to the English, the Dutch had become the dominant merchant carrier within Europe as well as between Europe and the colonies.

England's first formal response, mostly aimed at the Dutch, was the Navigation Act of 1651. It stated that English foreign trade was to be carried out only by English ships. As the American colonies were English, this was not a major issue for the Colonists.

In 1660 the second Navigation Act was passed, along with other laws in 1662, 1663, 1670, and 1673. These, at least on paper, should have been problematic for the colonists. They added the provisos that only English ships could transport goods from the colonies, only British citizens could trade with the colonies: and items produced in the colonies such as sugar, tobacco, and cotton wool could be only exported to British ports. Given that a major portion of the New England economy was tied up in the Triangular Trade, having to ship only through British ports would be an onerous restriction.

The laws, however, were simply ignored by the Colonists, making most American merchants smugglers. On a practical level, the English had no means of enforcing any of the laws.

By 1670 England tried to take more proactive steps to protect what they saw as their interests. In 1676, Edward Randolph was sent to Massachusetts to follow up on some complaints. After noting multiple American violations of the Crown's laws, he was appointed collector and surveyor of customs for all of New England.

Colonial opposition to Randolph's mission prompted him to return to England to seek the revocation of the Massachusetts Charter. (You may recall that the Charter was the legal base that enabled the New Englanders to easily circumvent much English control.)

After the English Civil Wars, things heated up further in 1685 when King James II was crowned. (James was also a Catholic, which also threatened and provoked the New England Puritans.) King James followed Randolph's advice and revoked the Massachusetts Charter. Massachusetts was joined with the other British territories from Delaware to Penobscot Bay (Maine) under the "Dominion of New England."

Sir Edmund Andros was then sent to Boston and installed as Governor. Several tax laws and duties were put into place, and the Navigation Acts were enforced. Prior attempts having failed, Andros forcibly established a Church of England chapel in 1688 (King's Chapel). He also tried to restrict town meetings. As you might imagine, these initiatives were not well received by the Puritan Colonists.

When it was learned that King James II had been deposed and succeeded by King William III and Queen Mary II in 1689, the Colonists revolted. Andros was captured, imprisoned (he did escape, but was recaptured) and returned to England in 1690.

The Colonists tried to resurrect the old Massachusetts Charter, but this effort was rejected. In 1691, the "Province of Massachusetts Bay" was put into place. Its new charter increased the province's territory along with other provisions.

The old charter had restricted voting to church members. With the new charter, the test became financial, not religious, meaning that Anglicans, and even Catholics, could vote. Government officials, including the governor and judges, were now appointed by the Crown, not elected. The net effect was that power was removed from the Colonists.

The new charter did retain a number of Colonist-favorable attributes, more than existed for other colonies. The General Court was still elected by the citizens, and the Court had power over appropriations (taxes). While the governor had veto power over the Court's laws, he was still much less powerful than in other colonies. This diminished power was to prove important in future disputes between the colonists and the Crown.

Disputes with England Escalate & the "Acts"

Entering the 1700's, Boston was the largest city in the colonies with a population of 7,000. In contrast, New York had almost 5,000 inhabitants, and Philadelphia 4,400. The total population of the colonies in 1700 was 275,000.

Boston was still a largely Puritan city, if not in absolute population, in culture and in practice. This meant that Bostonians were strong, independent, self-reliant and not tolerant of meddling by outside forces.

In 1700, Great Britain and the rest of Europe operated under a "mercantile system." All trade was supposed to be concentrated with the country or Empire of origin, with a sole goal of enriching the home country, its merchants and its government.

To support their mercantile policy, the British enacted a number of laws and Acts. Broadly, these fell into two categories: "revenue," which were designed to raise money; and "trade" which were to manage colonial trade. No matter the objective, the Acts were in direct conflict with Colonial interests, and were particularly offensive to the Boston and New England's Puritan-inspired psyche.

For as long as possible, the Colonists would actively ignore these laws, meaning that, in the eyes of British law, they were smugglers. The New Englanders became very good smugglers.

The first Act to inflame the Colonists was the Molasses Act (1733). This was put in place to protect the British West Indies by taxing the lower-priced molasses available from the French, Dutch, and Spanish West Indian islands. The molasses was used in New England for making rum. The Colonists occasionally paid the tax, but mostly it was ignored. The molasses was simply smuggled, or customs officials were bribed or intimidated.

In 1760, the Crown responded with the Writs of Assistance to help customs officers enforce the Navigation Acts, which had been in place since the 1660s. The Writs gave the customs agents carte blanche to search any place they wanted, without reason or probable cause. Further, searchers were not responsible for any damage they caused.

The Writs was a huge affront to Bostonian principles, not to mention the economic impact to merchants, many of whom were smugglers. There was also an argument that the Writs violated the fundamental rights of British subjects that dated back to the Magna Carta.

In 1761, the Writs were challenged by a group of 63 Boston merchants. The merchants were represented by Boston attorney James Otis, Jr., who had resigned his job as the Colony's chief prosecutor in disgust over the Writs. The case was presented at the Old State House.

Although Otis ultimately lost the case, his four hour performance was impassioned and impressive and placed him at the forefront of the early Revolutionary thought leaders. John Adams, who had heard Otis's argument, later wrote "Then and there the child Independence was born."

The Seven Years War (The French and Indian War, 1754 - treaty signed in 1763) doubled Britain's national debt. They needed to extract some amount of revenue from the colonies to help pay down the debt as well as to support the cost of maintaining a colonial military presence.

The first post Seven Years War act was the Sugar Act (1764), an updated version of the Molasses Act that also included taxes on wines, coffee, and other commodities. In addition to raising revenue, it was designed to constrain American trade with non-British partners.

The impact of the Sugar Act was particularly hurtful to New England as it made smuggling molasses much more risky. Also, the profit margin on rum was too small to support the tax. It was to be of less significance than subsequent Acts, but became a major "taxation without representation" issue in Boston.

Primary opposition to the Sugar Act was led by Samuel Adams and James Otis. Some fifty Boston merchants agreed to boycott British luxury goods and there was additional movement in Boston and New York to increase local goods production.

The Stamp Act (1765) required that Colonists pay a tax on many common printed materials, including legal documents, magazines and newspapers. This was highly offensive to the Colonists because it touched all levels of society. The Stamp Act brought about the first organized cross-colony coordinated resistance meeting when the "Stamp Act Congress" was held in New York in October of 1765.

At about this time the Sons of Liberty resistance group was formed. With their involvement, Boston was particularly virulent in its response to the Acts. Violence against the local tax collector and the smashing and looting of the house of then Lieutenant-Governor Hutchinson were just some of the altercations that occurred.

Intimidation forced many stamp tax distributors to resign their commissions, and the tax was never effectively collected. Both the Stamp and Sugar Acts were repealed in 1766.

The Townshend Acts (1767) taxed imported commodities such as paper, glass, and tea. The revenue was to be used to pay for governors and

Revere's "Sons of Liberty" Bowl at the Boston Museum of Fine Arts with Copley's wonderful portraits of Paul Revere, S. Adams, John Hancock & Dr. Joseph Warren

judges, previously paid from Colonial treasuries. This was to make the official effectively independent from Colonial influence.

In response, the Massachusetts House of Representatives sent a "Circular Letter" to other colonies asking for support. Boycotts were organized to pressure Parliament to repeal the acts. In Boston, resistance was so intense that customs officials requested military assistance to help enforce the trade regulations.

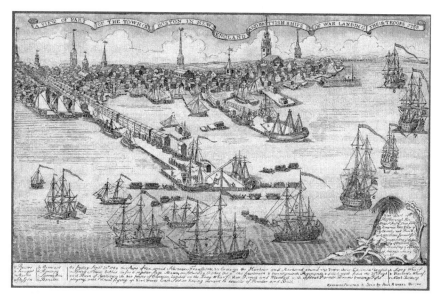

1768 Paul Revere engraving of British Troops landing in Boston

After the HMS Rodney, a 50-gun warship arrived in Boston, a riot ensued and 4 regiments of troops were sent to Boston to restore order. This was a large number of troops for a town of Boston's size - 4,000 soldiers for 16,000 townspeople, a ratio of 1:4.

The Boston Massacre

When the troops arrived, tensions between the English occupiers and the Colonists were understandably high. Two of the regiments were removed the following year, but the 14th and 29th remained - and so did the tension.

Making things worse was the fact that the Boston economy was in recession, and to pick up extra cash some of the underpaid British troops were competing with locals for already scarce work.

In late February of 1770, an 11 year old boy named Christopher Seider was shot and killed in the North End by Ebenezer Richardson, an employee of the Custom Office. Richardson had tried to aid a Loyalist whose shop was targeted by Townshend Act boycotters opposing the sale of British merchandise. In the ensuing altercation, Richardson fired his gun into the crowd, killing Seider and wounding another protester.

Samuel Adams proclaimed Seider a martyr and orchestrated an elaborate funeral, with over 2,000 people (of a total Boston population of about 16,000) in attendance. This was a massive event that stoked the already tense emotions.

On the cold, snowy night of March 5, just a few days after Seider's death, British Private Hugh White stood on guard duty outside the Custom House. Edward Garrick, a young wig maker's apprentice called out to a passing British officer, Captain Lieutenant John Goldfinch, that Goldfinch had not paid a bill. Insults were exchanged between White, Garrick and Goldfinch, and White ended up hitting Garrick on the head with his musket.

A crowd gathered and Church bells were rung. The ringing of Church bells usually indicated a fire, and Boston had a history of devastating fires, so more people turned out. Snowballs and other debris were hurled at Private White.

At this point, over 50 taunting Bostonians had gathered. The local barracks were alerted and a Captain Preston, together with a group of soldiers with fixed bayonets, proceeded to relieve White. Henry Knox, a local bookseller (who would later become the chief artillery officer of the Continental Army), tried to counsel Captain Preston to diffuse tensions. Instead the soldiers loaded their muskets and arrayed themselves around the Custom House steps.

The crowd now numbered three to four hundred. There were shouts of "fire" and the pelting of the soldiers continued. One of the soldiers was knocked down and a Bostonian clubbed the soldier and Captain Preston.

Close-up from Paul Revere's Engraving of the Boston Massacre

Although Preston never gave the order to fire, shots rang out and eleven Bostonians were hit. Three died immediately - rope maker Samuel Gray, mariner James Caldwell, and a mixed-race Indian-African named Crispus

Attucks. Samuel Maverick, a seventeen year old apprentice ivory turner died later that night and Irish immigrant Patrick Carr died two weeks later.

Governor Hutchinson managed to quiet down the crowd by promising an investigation. Over the next few weeks, under tremendous pressure from the townspeople to avoid further bloodshed, both regiments were moved to Castle William, a fort in Boston harbor.

The promised investigation began the following day. Captain Preston, the eight soldiers involved, and four civilians were indicted for murder.

The trials started in October of that year. The local government was determined to give the soldiers a fair trial, both to avoid British retribution and to avoid alienating moderates from the Patriot cause.

Prominent attorneys John Adams and Josiah Quincy II were appointed as defense counsel. (John Adams was Samuel Adam's cousin, later a signer of the Declaration of Independence and the 2nd President of the United States.) Massachusetts Solicitor General Samuel Quincy (Josiah's older brother) and attorney Robert Treat Paine (also signer of the Declaration of Independence) were the prosecutors.

Captain Preston was acquitted when the jury was convinced that he had not given an order to fire on the crowd. Adams made an articulate argument that the soldiers were threatened by the mob were merely defending themselves. The jury agreed and six of the soldiers were acquitted outright. The remaining two soldiers were convicted of manslaughter. Due to an arcane law in effect at the time called "Benefit of Clergy," the convicted soldiers received a reduced sentence. Their thumbs were branded with an "M" in open court.

The Townshend Acts were repealed in April 1770 and things were relatively quiet in Boston until 1773.

The Tea Act and the Boston Tea Party

To web-translate The Tea Act through the Response to the Acts (password required):
http://www.stevestravelguide.com/?p=1383

In May 1773 everything changed with the passage of the Tea Act. The Tea Act gave a bailout to the struggling East India Tea Company, providing them the ability to import tea directly through a few selected consignees. This cut out traditional Colonial middlemen, hurt local importers, and gave the East India Tea a competitive price advantage, hurting competitive merchants.

The Tea Act set off a firestorm of protests in the colonies – not the least was the no taxation without representation concern. Coordinated cross-colony opposition was set up. Consignees were harassed, and in New York, Philadelphia, and Charleston there were successful efforts to prevent tea from being landed.

Boston failed to stop the tea as Governor Hutchinson refused to back down - perhaps having two sons who were consignees influenced his thinking. Four ships loaded with tea were on their way to Boston.

The first ship, the Dartmouth, arrived in Boston in November 1773. A clock started to tick when the Dartmouth arrived as British law required that the tea be unloaded within twenty days and duties paid or customs officials could confiscate the cargo.

Resistance to the tea's landing was led by the Sons of Liberty, of which Samuel Adams was a leading member. Adams called a meeting at Faneuil Hall to be held for November 29. Thousands of citizens showed up and the meeting had to be moved to the much larger Old South Meeting House.

The outcome was the passage of a resolution similar to what had been passed in Philadelphia. It called for the Dartmouth's captain to send the ship back and not pay the duty. Governor Hutchinson vetoed the resolution.

Two additional ships, the Eleanor and the Beaver had arrived by mid-December. The fourth ship, the William, was lost in a storm.

On the last day of the Dartmouth's 20 day deadline there was another gathering at the Old South Meeting House. The over 5,000 Patriots gathered again tried to convince Governor Hutchinson to back down. Again, they were unsuccessful.

When it was learned that Governor Hutchinson refused to let the ships leave, Samuel Adams said "This meeting can do nothing further to save the country." Some stories have Adam's statement as a prearranged signal for the tea party to begin. Other accounts suggest that Adams was trying to restore order.

Boston Tea Party Lithograph by Sarony & Major

No matter, a group of about 100 men disguised as Mohawk Indians went to Griffin's Wharf where the ships were docked. They boarded them, and carefully, so as not to disturb the non-tea merchandise, dumped the entire cargo of 342 chests of tea into Boston harbor. This amounted to some 45 tons of tea with a present day value of over $1,700,000.

Tea Party Aftermath - The Intolerable Acts

Great Britain responded to the Tea Party in 1774 with the Intolerable Acts, also known as the Coercive Acts. Four of the acts were punitive and designed to make a direct example of Massachusetts in the hope that resistance across the colonies would diminish. The fifth act, the Quebec Act, instituted reforms favorable to the French Catholics in the region to help them feel better about being British subjects. It also enlarged the boundaries of the Province of Quebec.

Lieutenant General Thomas Gage was sent to Boston as military Governor to replace Governor Hutchinson. Gage was popular on both sides of the Atlantic and deemed the best man to handle the crisis and to enforce the Acts.

The Boston Port Act shut down the port of Boston until the East India Company was repaid for the tea dumped into the harbor and the Royal treasury paid for lost customs duties that would have been paid on the tea.

Boston was closed to all shipping and the Royal Navy patrolled the harbor to enforce a blockade. The customs house was moved to Salem, about 40 miles north of Boston.

The Port Act was devastating in New England, and nobody, Loyalist or Patriot, was happy with it as it punished everyone. In Boston, almost all goods – even staples like food and firewood - were brought in via the harbor because the land path to the mainland was Boston Neck. Boston Neck was a tiny causeway only a hundred or so feet wide, windswept and wet during high tide. It was often shut entirely during inclement weather, especially during winter.

The Port Act was a financial disaster as without shipping there were no jobs. Further, what little there was to buy was very expensive. The residents did receive contributions of food, supplies and money from colonies as far away as Georgia and Nova Scotia. Despite this help, Boston's population dropped from 16,000 to 3,500.

The Massachusetts Government Act undercut the Massachusetts Charter and put government in the hands of the British. Prior to this Act, Massachusetts had been unique among the colonies in its ability to elect members of its governing council. Now, the British had the power to appoint the council. Many previously elected civil offices were now appointed by the Royal Governor.

Town meetings, with the exception of one annual meeting, could not be held without the governor's consent. Governor Thomas Gage used the Government Act to cancel the Massachusetts General Court (the State Legislature).

The Administration of Justice Act was supposed to ensure that Crown officials accused of crimes were treated fairly – independent from the prejudices of local juries. It allowed the governor to move a trial to another colony or even to Britain. Witnesses for both the prosecution and defense were required to attend, and were supposed to be compensated for their expenses. In practice, as most Colonists could not afford to take time off of work to attend a trial, this was a farce.

The Quartering Act tried to make it simpler to house British troops. Prior to this Act, the colonies were supposed to provide housing for soldiers, but in reality made it very difficult for the British to do so. The new Act allowed a governor to house soldiers in other buildings if other suitable quarters could not be found. In practice, only empty buildings were used so the Act's impact was minimal.

Response to The Acts

Even though the Acts were largely targeted at Boston and New England, they presented problems for all the colonies. All colonists now feared that their status could be changed by an arbitrary legislative fiat of Parliament.

In Massachusetts, Patriots responded by creating the Massachusetts Provincial Congress, which operated a shadow government for the state. The Provincial Congress took on all the powers necessary to run the province including taxing, purchasing, and raising the militia.

John Hancock became the Provincial Congress president, and he ordered that taxes be paid to the Provincial Congress, not the British government. Congress also authorized that a core of Minutemen be available from the local militia that would be ready for battle "on the shortest notice." The Congress frequently had to move from town to town to avoid Royal capture.

In denunciation of the Intolerable Acts, the Suffolk Resolves were passed by the leaders of Suffolk County in Massachusetts in the fall of 1774 (Boston was the primary city in Suffolk County). The Resolves were authored by Patriot leader Dr. Joseph Warren.

The Resolves were delivered by Paul Revere to the First Continental Congress in Philadelphia. They were enforced and directly influenced documents the Congress produced.

> *"British oppression has effaced the boundaries of the several colonies; the distinctions between Virginians, Pennsylvanians and New Englanders are no more. I am not a Virginian, but an American."* Patrick Henry, the famous Virginia orator-Patriot to the delegation at the First Continental Congress. What had been a loose collection of independent Colonies was now beginning to think of themselves as united, with a common cause.

The First Continental Congress, which included delegates from all of the original thirteen colonies except for Georgia, met in Philadelphia in September of 1774 to coordinate the cross-colony response to the Acts. The Congress was built upon the Committees of Correspondence structure. The first Committee was started by Samuel Adams and Joseph Warren in Massachusetts in 1772.

The Committees of Correspondence, consisting of only Patriots, had become the de facto Colonial shadow governments. These Committees provided loose inter-colony coordination starting in 1773. A total of about 7,000 to 8,000 Patriots served on these Committees, at the colonial and local levels. Membership included a who's who of the Patriot leaders.

The First Continental Congress had two primary outcomes. The first was a boycott of British goods. In 1775, imports from Britain were cut by 97 percent over the prior year. The Congress also agreed that if the Acts were not repealed, the colonies' exports to Britain would cease in September, 1775. (As the Revolutionary War started in April of 1775, the export boycott became meaningless.) The Congress also urged the formation of militias.

The second major accomplishment of the First Congress was to schedule the Second Continental Congress for May of 1775. The Second Continental Congress became the governing body for the war effort and adopted the Declaration of Independence on July 4, 1776. It raised armies, directed strategy, appointed diplomats, negotiated treaties – e.g., operated as the de facto government of what was to become the United States.

The Second Congress's actions were legitimized by the drafting of the Articles of Confederation, which was finished in late 1777. Ratification of the Articles by the states was completed in 1779. The Articles of Confederation legally established the United States of America.

Paul Revere's Ride

To web-translate Paul Revere's Ride through the Battles of Lexington & Concord (password required):

http://www.stevestravelguide.com/?p=1391

Governor Thomas Gage believed that one path needed to enforce the Intolerable Acts was to eliminate the Patriots' ability to fight by seizing their military stores. In September of 1774, he staged a successful raid to remove a large supply of gun powder stored at the Powder House near Winter Hill, in Somerville, about 8 miles from Boston.

The Patriots were caught flatfooted, and the powder was captured and removed. In response, they formalized the Minuteman structure as well as a system of rapid "alarm and muster" to facilitate the notification and deployment of militias in the event of an emergency.

The Minuteman structure had local militias keep a quarter of their personnel equipped and ready to march on immediate notice. Additionally, supplies of materials and munitions were moved to safer locations farther away from the coast – to Worcester and Concord.

In early December, Britain decided to outlaw the export of arms and powder to North America. On December 14, Gage authorized a mission to seize the stores at Fort William and Mary in Portsmouth, New Hampshire, some 60 miles north of Boston. Warned by Patriot messenger Paul Revere, the stores at the fort were seized by the Patriots. (This was really the first organized military action of the Revolution, not Lexington and Concord.)

In late February of 1775, a force of about 240 British regulars was sent to seize weapons stored in Salem, Massachusetts, about 10 miles north of Boston. This expedition was thwarted by local action without bloodshed.

On April 14, 1775, Gage finally received instructions from London to disarm the rebels and imprison the rebel leaders – especially Samuel Adams and John Hancock. In preparation, Gage had previously sent out scouting patrols to reconnoiter potential marching routes to both Concord and Worcester. Worcester was deemed too dangerous to attack, so the target had to be Concord. The mission needed to be kept a surprise.

On the morning of April 18, Gage sent a mounted patrol to intercept Patriot messengers who might spread the alarm. On the evening of that day, the commander of the expedition, Lieutenant Colonel Francis Smith, was given the previously secret orders. He was to destroy the Patriot supplies stored at Concord.

In total, the expedition consisted of about 700 men and was the elite of the British troops in Boston. Smith's executive officer was Major John Pitcairn, who would command the 10 companies of light infantry, the most athletic and mobile troops. The remaining 11 companies were grenadiers, the largest and strongest men.

The troops were woken up at about 9 PM on the 18th, and assembled at Boston Common. Starting at midnight, they were ferried over the Charles River to Cambridge. There were not enough barges for everyone, so it took two trips.

Once on the Cambridge side of the river, the troops had to wade through muddy, waste deep water to get to shore. So, this soggy group of soldiers was already tired and grumpy at 2 AM when they began their 17 mile march for Concord.

What was supposed to be a secret expedition was pretty well understood by the Patriot intelligence machine. London sources had even sent them information on Gage's orders by fast ship - they reached the Patriots before Gage had seen them.

By April 8th, most of the important Patriots had left Boston and Paul Revere had delivered a warning of suspicious British behavior to Concord. This enabled some of Concord's arsenal to be distributed to neighboring towns. The Patriots were also briefed on the April 19th expedition by someone inside Gage's inner circle, likely his Connecticut-born wife Martha, who had known Patriot sympathies.

There was also Patriot knowledge of the advanced party of British troops that had been sent to waylay messengers. It was thought that the primary British mission, however, was to capture Samuel Adams and John Hancock, as Concord was deemed too far away.

The only thing that was really a mystery was whether the British were going to march "by land" - over Boston Neck, or "by sea" - transported across the harbor.

In preparation for the British march, Revere pre-arranged with Robert Newman, the sexton of the (Old) North Church, to alert Patriots in Charlestown as soon as the British path out of Boston was understood. One lantern hung in the church's steeple would indicate the land route, two the water route.

Newman worked with two other Patriots to devise the plan. It is interesting to note that the North Church was Anglican with a Loyalist rector, which made using it exceedingly dangerous for Revere and Newman.

Dr. Joseph Warren, the senior Patriot leader remaining in town, coordinated the activities within Boston. When he learned of the British march from his source, he summoned Paul Revere and William Dawes, sending them to warn Adams and Hancock and alarm the local towns. (William Dawes was a local tanner, and although not as well-known as Revere, an ardent Patriot.)

Getting Revere and Dawes out of Boston undetected was not simple as the British guarded all paths - land and sea. To make sure that the message got through, Warren asked Revere to cross the harbor to Charlestown (by sea) and ride from there, and Dawes to ride through Boston Neck (by land), where he was known to the sentries. Both men were given written messages describing what was known of the British sortie.

Dawes is rumored to have talked his way through the guards at the Boston Neck gate. (In another account, he got out just prior to the guards receiving orders to stop all travel.) No matter what really happened, his exit from Boston took luck and skill. Once through the gate, he managed to elude patrols and make his way into Cambridge then on to the road to Lexington.

Revere's path through Charlestown needed preparation as well as luck. In addition to planning the lantern signals with Newman and the Charlestown Patriots, getting across the river was extremely hazardous.

When he left Warren's surgery at about 10 PM, Revere alerted Newman to hang two lanterns. The lights were seen by the Charlestown Patriots, who sent off their own messenger (who never got through), found a horse for Revere, and went to the water to wait for his arrival.

Revere left his house about 10:15 PM, met up with two friends who would help get him across the river, uncovered a hidden boat, and started rowing to Charlestown. The next challenge was getting past the 64 gun British warship HMS Somerset, which was anchored to stop all traffic between Boston and Charlestown. And the moon was almost full.

Miraculously, Revere made it across without incident and met the Charlestown Patriots, and picked up Brown Beauty, the mare they had selected for him. By all accounts, Brown Beauty was an excellent choice.

Being careful to avoid British patrols, which included one harrowing chase that forced a detour to Medford, Revere rode through the present-day towns of Somerville, Medford and Arlington on his way to Lexington.

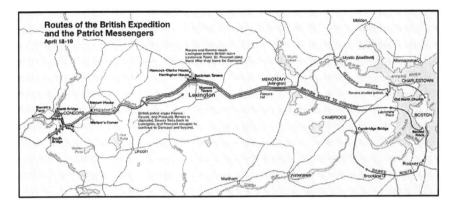

National Park Service Map of Revere's Ride & Battles of Lexington & Concord

Revere warned Patriots along the way and they followed the well planned "alarm and muster" scheme. The system was so effective that Patriots in towns 25 miles (40 km) from Boston were aware that the British march was under way even before the soggy, tired British troops began their march from Cambridge at 2 AM.

In Lexington, Hancock and Adams were staying at the home of one of Hancock's relatives, Reverend Jonas Clarke. (The house is now called the Hancock-Clarke House, just a short walk from Lexington Green and open to tourists). Around midnight Revere arrived at the house, with Dawes arriving about ½ hour later. Hancock and Adams were informed of the British march and objectives, and encouraged to leave quickly.

Revere and Dawes continued along the road to Concord accompanied by Samuel Prescott, a young doctor who happened to be in Lexington courting a lady friend. They were captured by a British patrol in Lincoln, about ½ ways between Lexington and Concord. Prescott's familiarity with the local terrain helped him to escape by jumping his horse over a wall.

Prescott was the only one to reach Concord. Dawes initially got away but was recaptured when he was thrown by his horse. The British had several other captives from their night's work.

Revere was questioned at gunpoint by the British soldiers. He told them of the British army's movement from Boston - he knew more than the soldiers did - and that British troops would be in danger if they approached Lexington because of the large number of Patriot militia that were assembling. (Revere exaggerated, hoping to keep the British out of Lexington to give more time for Adams and Hancock to escape.) He succeeded in agitating his captors.

As the soldiers and their prisoners proceeded toward Lexington, gunshots were heard. Asked to explain the shots, Revere replied that it was a signal to "alarm the country". Another of the Patriot prisoners said "The bell's a ringing! The town's alarmed and you're all dead men."

Believing they needed to move quickly to warn the troops marching from Boston, the patrol released the captives so they could travel faster. Revere's horse, Brown Beauty, was confiscated (never to be seen again) and he and the other prisoners were released. The former Patriot captives then hiked towards Lexington Green.

Before reaching the Green, Revere checked to make sure Adams and Hancock had left. Finding them still at Reverend Clarke's house, he participated in encouraging them to flee.

After their departure, Revere helped hide a trunk of Hancock's papers. Revere and another Patriot carried the trunk past the line of Patriot militia that had assembled on Lexington Green just as the British arrived.

Lexington and Concord - "Shot Heard Round the World"

The first British troops to reach Lexington were an advance guard of light infantry under the command of Major Pitcairn. They approached Lexington at sunrise, about 5 AM, the same time Paul Revere was helping to hide Hancock's trunk.

A group of about 80 Lexington militiamen under the command of Captain Parker, a veteran of the French and Indian War, waited for the British to arrive. Parker understood that the militiamen were over-matched and decided not to try and detain the British. The militia would, however, make a showing, and then let the British pass.

When the advance guard arrived, a British lieutenant called out for the militia to disperse and according to some reports may have said "lay down your arms, you damned rebels!" Parker instead told his men to disperse and go home, but some may not have heard him and left only slowly. All retained their arms.

Nobody knows who fired the first shot as neither Parker nor Pitcairn ordered their men to fire, but a shot was heard. The excited British then fired a volley and charged the Patriots with their bayonets. Eight Massachusetts Patriots were killed and ten were wounded. There was only one minor British casualty.

Under duress, the British commander, Colonel Smith finally managed to restore order. He permitted the British troops to fire a victory volley, then the march to Concord proceeded. Colonel Smith also sent a messenger back to Boston to request that the British relief column, which was supposedly assembled and ready to march, be sent.

At about 7 AM, the British arrived at Concord. One group of troops was sent to secure the South Bridge entrance to town, and another larger group was sent north to look for some supplies that British spies had identified were hidden past North Bridge. Of the northern group, one contingent secured the North Bridge, the other went to search for the supplies.

(As the British arrived at Concord, the Patriot militia decided their force was insufficient to confront them and had retreated to a hill just outside of town across North Bridge.)

In town, the British found and disabled a few heavy cannons, destroyed some food, and dumped some musket balls into the millpond. Several gun carriages were discovered and burned, with the fire inadvertently spreading to the village's meetinghouse, leaving smoke hovering over the town.

At 9 AM the assembled Patriot troops saw the smoke and assumed the whole town had been set on fire. The concerned Patriots then advanced towards North Bridge. The British troops that had been securing the bridge retreated to the side closest to town.

The British fired a ragged volley into the approaching Patriots, killing two and wounding four. The Patriots fired back. In the exchange, four of eight British officers and sergeants were wounded; of the privates at least three were killed or mortally wounded; nine others were wounded.

The British retreated into town to rest, recall and wait for their other troops, and treat the wounded. They started back towards Lexington at about noon, a journey of about five miles. The road between Concord and Lexington was narrow at places, crossed several bridges, and was surrounded by hills.

By this time, 2,000 Patriot militia had gathered and decided to ambush the British as they marched. Contrary to the legend of the solitary Patriot behind a wall, the Patriots fought in a coordinated fashion at company and even regimental strength. The fighting was brutal and hotly contested.

[The weapon of the day was the musket, which had an effective range of about 50 yards (42 meters). Close order combat was therefore required for much damage to be done. In spite of anecdotes to the contrary, there is no evidence of any rifles being used by either side during this battle.]

Battles continued the entire way back to Lexington with considerable casualties - mostly British. By the time the British approached Lexington at 2PM, their ammunition was almost exhausted and panic was setting in.

When Lexington was finally in sight, the retreating British troops gratefully found the Boston relief column set up on hills surrounding the town center. The relief column had deployed two cannons which began a covering fire, dispersing the pursuing Patriots and giving the retreating column time to reach safety.

After resting in Lexington until about 3:30 PM, the British set out toward Boston. The Colonial militia surrounded the British, sniping and ambushing as their enemy passed. The British sent out flankers to protect the column and conducted as orderly a fighting withdrawal as possible.

Fighting was particularly heavy in Menotomy (present day Arlington) where both sides lost about ½ of those killed during the entire day. This amounted to 25 killed and 9 wounded for the Patriots, and 40 killed and 80 wounded for the British. Some homes were used by the Patriots as sniping positions, forcing the British into house to house fighting to clear them out. Multiple atrocities were committed by the frustrated British troops.

When the retreating British column finally reached Charlestown, it was almost dark. They were reinforced from Boston and protected by the guns of the HMS Somerset – the same ship that Paul Revere had rowed silently past almost 24 hours before.

The ferrying of wounded British troops to Boston took all night. The Patriots withdrew to Cambridge.

Total Patriot casualties for the day were 49 killed, 34 wounded and 5 missing - 18 of whom fell during the initial clash at Lexington. British casualties totaled 273 - 73 killed and 174 wounded, with 26 declared missing.

The Siege of Boston

To web-translate the Siege of Boston through the Charles Bulfinch Era (password required):

http://www.stevestravelguide.com/?p=1394

After the Battles of Lexington and Concord, Patriots continued to march to Boston from as far as Connecticut, Rhode Island and New Hampshire. Their numbers ultimately reached 20,000. A cordon was placed around Boston - effectively blocking the city from land access and placing it under siege.

The only way for the British to get supplies into or out of Boston was via the harbor. Most Loyalists moved into Boston for protection, and many Patriots chose to leave the city.

The British fortified the primary hills in the city and abandoned their positions on Charlestown. On the south, Dorchester Heights, which had a commanding view of the harbor and city, was left undefended as there were insufficient troops. General Gage requested reinforcements.

In spite of the Royal Navy's command of the harbor and sea routes, supplies within Boston were short and prices rose rapidly. Meat was scarce and the horses needed hay. The Patriots effectively raided British supplies on the harbor islands and in one celebrated incident, the British Schooner Diana ran aground and was destroyed.

With their active spy networks, the Patriot forces generally had good information about what was happening in the city. General Gage had no effective intelligence of rebel activities.

After hearing of the fights at Lexington and Concord, Benedict Arnold, a wealthy Connecticut merchant, convinced the Massachusetts Committee of Safety to fund an expedition to capture Fort Ticonderoga. At the southern tip of Lake Champlain, Ticonderoga housed a large number of cannon and military supplies that would be of use to the Patriots.

Along with Ethan Allen and his Green Mountain Boys, Arnold captured Ticonderoga on May 10. The captured cannons were later hauled to Boston to be used by the Patriots on Dorchester Heights.

The Second Continental Congress started their meeting in Philadelphia soon after the battles at Lexington and Concord. Massachusetts delegates included Samuel Adams and John Hancock, the latter serving as president.

One of the major accomplishments of the Second Continental Congress was to provide for a real Continental Army for purposes of common defense. The troops already in place outside of Boston (then 22,000 troops) and New York (5,000) were to make up the first recruits. George Washington was elected Commander-in-Chief by a unanimous vote.

Washington left Philadelphia for Boston on June 21, but he did not arrive until July 3rd, weeks after the Battle of Bunker Hill in Charlestown.

The Battle of Bunker Hill

After Lexington and Concord, the requested British reinforcements trickled in, finally bringing British strength to about 6,000 by late May. Three Major Generals - William Howe, Henry Clinton, and John Burgoyne were among those sent to encourage Lieutenant General Gage to take more aggressive action.

The plan the British evolved was to shore up the weak points by taking Dorchester Heights to the south and Charlestown to the north before moving on the main rebel headquarters in Cambridge, to the west. The date for the taking of Dorchester Heights, was set for early on June 18, a Sunday, so many Colonials would be attending services at their meeting house.

The rebels had picked up rumors of British activity, and the British plan was described in detail by a reliable source on June 14th. The Patriot Committee of Safety met on the 15th to develop a response and decided to fortify Bunker Hill in Charlestown. Dorchester Heights was not deemed defensible because the Patriots lacked adequate heavy artillery.

Colonel William Prescott was ordered to march to Charlestown to fortify Bunker Hill. On the night of June 16 he led about 1,200 men to Charlestown with entrenching equipment. For reasons that have never been clarified, he decided to fortify Breed's instead of Bunker Hill. Breed's Hill was closer to Boston, but it was also potentially tougher to defend as it could be surrounded and cut off from the rear.

When the British awoke on the morning of June 17, they saw the rebel works erected on Breed's Hill. Firing on the rebel fortifications began almost immediately after sunrise from a British frigate anchored in the harbor.

The British generals met to consider their options. Their desire was to respond quickly and sweep the Americans off Charlestown before the Americans could dig-in and reinforce. The British generals have been unfairly criticized by many historians for their course of action. Given the constraints, their options were actually quite limited.

To land troops behind the rebel redoubt, surround them and cut them off from retreat was impractical. The British did not have the flat bottom landing craft needed to navigate Charlestown's marshy coastline. The only craft they had were the long boats from the men-of-war in the harbor. Planning, equipping and executing an amphibious operation is complex and takes time.

Because the British wanted to strike the same day, (some counseled a more complex plan that would not be ready until the following day), what they chose to do was an acceptable decision.

General Howe was given command of the expedition. The plan was to land a 1,600 man force on the northeast tip of Charlestown, Moulton's Point, and sweep the rebels off the peninsula. The main assault would sweep around the Colonial left flank and take the redoubt from the rear. A diversionary assault would be aimed at the redoubt to hold the rebels in place. Final adjustments would be made on the ground prior to the assault once the rebel defenses were seen close up.

The day was very hot, by some accounts as much as 95 degrees. The Patriots, having worked all night, were tired, hungry, and thirsty. They did not have much ammunition.

Superior Patriot officers also present in Charlestown included Dr. Joseph Warren (President of the Committee of Safety and Provincial Congress, and also recently appointed a Major General in the Army)

Old North Church as seen today from the site of the Patriot Redoubt on Breed's (Bunker) Hill

and Major General Israel Putnam, then second in command of all the Colonial troops surrounding Boston. Both generals were offered command on the field by Colonel Prescott, but both declined.

In preparation for the assault, the British shelled Patriot positions from frigates anchored in the harbor and a heavy battery of 24 pound cannon that had been set up on Copp's Hill in the North End.

About 1,600 British troops were ferried across and ready by about 2 PM. Upon seeing the rebel deployments, Howe ordered the 700 reinforcements waiting in Boston to be brought over, delaying the assault until about 3 PM.

On their right, the Patriots manned the redoubt on the top of Breed's Hill. Their line then ran north until it hit the Mystic River. There were fleches (small angled field works) running down the hill that connected the redoubt with a breastwork of stones and fence rails that ran to the river. The breastwork was to become known as the "rail fence."

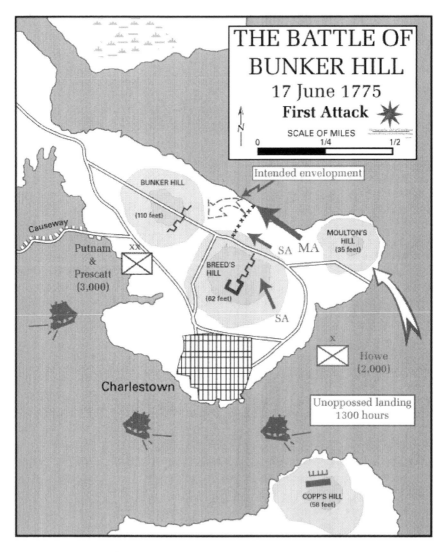

US Military Academy Map of the First Assault

Colonel John Stark (a feisty French & Indian war veteran commanding troops from New Hampshire), commanding the troops at the breastwork, put a firing marker stake about 50 yards out (46 meters) in front of the breastworks. The Patriots were to hold their fire until the British reached the firing marker.

Prior to the attack, the British troops were receiving sniper fire from

Colonials holed up in the abandoned town of Charlestown. The British response was to burn down the town by shelling it with red-hot cannon balls. The town was dry and ignited quickly.

The battle was to be one of the most watched in history with spectators outnumbering participants. It would be watched from the north, across the Mystic River in Chelsea, and the south, from Boston.

Visually, it must have been spectacular. The smoke from burning Charlestown billowed black and reportedly almost blocked out the sun. The red and white ranks of the British troops advanced on the hill. White puffs of smoke emanated from the ships' cannons and Copp's Hill.

The first British attack, consisting of elite light infantry and grenadiers, was aimed at the breastwork and rail fence with just a feint towards the redoubt. The Colonists held their fire until the British reached the marker ("Don't fire until you see the whites of their eyes," was reportedly ordered by Prescott) and then the opened fire. The front lines of the British infantry just melted away. The Colonists continued to pour in fire until the British turned and fled.

The second assault was concentrated on the redoubt with a feint against the rail fence. It had the same outcome as the first assault. The British tumbled back in disarray.

The third assault concentrated on the redoubt with only a small demonstration at the rail fence. It was successful, but the British still endured significant punishment.

With the Patriots running out of ammunition, the redoubt was finally breached. Fighting was hand to hand, British bayonet to Colonial clubbed musket, with the advantage decidedly British. The Colonials had to flee down the peninsula to escape.

Technically, the British won the battle as they forced a Patriot retreat and took control of Charlestown. But, they had lost heavily - about 1,000 casualties of the 2,300 soldiers engaged. 226 had been killed outright and approximately 250 of the 828 wounded were to die as a result of their wounds. Major John Pitcairn received a mortal wound. It took until the following morning to complete the transfer of the wounded and remaining soldiers back to Boston.

Of the 2,500 to 3,000 Colonials involved (although no more than 1,500 were involved at any one time, and likely ½ that number at the conclusion of the battle), there were between 500-600 casualties. Of those, approximately 130 died on the field and an additional 30 were captured. The dead included Dr. Joseph Warren, a major blow to the Patriot leadership.

British Lieutenant General Gage was recalled three days after his battle report arrived in England, but he did not receive his orders until September 26. He was replaced by Major General William Howe.

George Washington & the Siege is Lifted

On July 3, George Washington arrived to take charge of the new Continental Army. His headquarters was set up in Cambridge, in a house that later became the home of William Wadsworth Longfellow.

The Army Washington inherited was nothing like the organized, discipline troops that he would need. Many enlistments were expiring and discipline was lax. The task of recruiting and molding the troops and leadership into something that resembled an Army was daunting, and was continued throughout the fall.

About 2,000 of the new recruits were riflemen from Pennsylvania, Maryland and Virginia. The new troops were to provide the first long-range rifle fire the British would experience.

Over the summer, defenses were improved by both sides and there were several sorties with some loss of life. There was, however, nothing of consequence. In September, Washington began planning for two moves: to invade Quebec, and to launch an attack on Boston.

1,100 troops were sent to attack Quebec under the command of Benedict Arnold - in what was to be a disastrous campaign. Washington then called a council of war to build consensus for an amphibious attack on Boston. The attack plan was unanimously rejected, and the plans called off.

Strengthening of defenses by both sides continued and more skirmishes took place on both land and sea, most with little effect. In late November, the Patriots captured a British brigantine bound for Boston along with some desperately needed military stores. (The Patriots were so low on gunpowder that some were armed with spears in case of British attack.) The Patriots, however, were well supplied with food, the British were not.

The standoff continued throughout the fall and winter. The Boston winter of 1775-76 was particularly tough on the British as they were completely surrounded and the only way in or out of the city was via the harbor. Supply via the harbor was becoming increasingly difficult as Patriot privateers were becoming more active.

Wood for heating was scarce and virtually all the trees and many buildings in Boston – including the Old North Meeting House in North Square - were used for firewood. The British troops were so hungry that many were ready to desert. Scurvy was rampant and there was a major smallpox epidemic.

In November, Henry Knox presented General Washington with a plan to transport heavy cannon captured at Fort Ticonderoga to Boston. Washington appointed Knox a colonel and accepted his mission. Leading a harrowing expedition across the frozen Hudson and Connecticut Rivers dragging the cannon on oxen-pulled sleds, Knox arrived back in Boston at the end of January, 1776 with 60 tons of heavy artillery. Some of the Ticonderoga cannons had a size and range not previously available.

On the night of March 5th, in a stealth-clothed operation, Washington moved some of the heavy cannon and several thousand men to fortify

Dorchester Heights. The ground on the heights was frozen, forcing Washington's men to bring much of the fortifying material (branches, logs, etc.) with them.

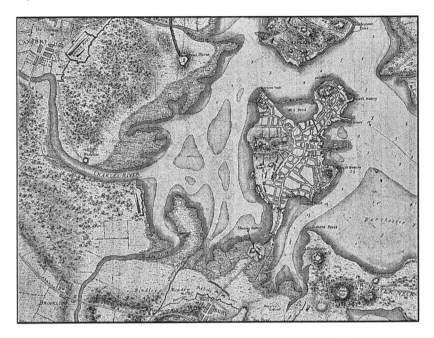

Close-up of 1775 Map Showing Dorchester, Charlestown, and Boston

When the British awoke on March 6th, Washington had a commanding position overlooking the city, with the British fleet within range of the American heavy guns. A two hour British cannon barrage had no effect because as the British guns could not reach the American guns on Dorchester Heights. An assault was planned, but was canceled due to a storm.

Being in an untenable position, the British elected to leave Boston. On March 8th, Washington received a communication indicating that the British would not destroy the town if they were allowed to leave unmolested. Washington accepted the terms.

Over the next week or so, the British tried to destroy anything that would be of use to the Patriots, loaded up their ships, and waited for favorable winds to sail. Early on March 17th, about 120 ships set sail for Halifax, Nova Scotia with about 9,000 British troops and over 1,000 Loyalists and their families.

Spearheaded by troops who had already had smallpox, Washington's men entered Boston to find it a shambles. In addition to the trees and buildings destroyed for firewood, the Old South Church had been turned into a stable, private homes were serving as hospitals, and public buildings had been defaced. From a pre-war population of 20,000, Boston's population was down to around 3,500.

The Siege of Boston was over.

After the Revolution

Economic conditions remained hard even after the war ended in 1783. Inflation was high, qualified workers were scarce, and the machinery and dockyards that had remained largely idle since before Lexington and Concord were in a state of disrepair. When a period of deflation set in, rural areas were particularly hard hit.

Things in Boston improved after the new Constitution was put into place in 1787. Trade with the Caribbean Islands increased, with New England codfish, whale oil and manufactured goods were traded for cocoa, sugar, molasses, and tobacco.

By the late 1790's, trade expanded to South America. When the Napoleonic wars between England and France made trading with Europe hazardous, New Englanders expanded their markets to include Rio de Janeiro, the West Coast of North America, and China.

By 1790, Boston's population was back up to 18,000, by 1800 it had reached 25,000, and by 1810 it had reached 30,000. With the growing population came overcrowding and the desire of the more affluent population to move from the crowded downtown area around Faneuil Hall (Dock-Square) into the South and West Ends, then Beacon Hill.

The Charles Bulfinch Era

The single, most influential person in structuring Boston's expansion was architect Charles Bulfinch. Bulfinch was born in 1763, attended Boston Latin and studied at Harvard College. During a two-year tour of Europe he was influenced by the beautiful town planning in Paris and the work of Sir Christopher Wren in England.

Upon returning to Boston in 1787, Bulfinch began to apply his European ideas to Boston architecture and planning. His designs followed the Federal style of red brick with classic balance and simplicity. Much of his work may still be seen on and around the Freedom Trail.

Bulfinch began sketches for a new state capitol as early as 1787. He was officially selected as the architect for the project in 1795 when town purchased pastureland on Beacon Hill that once belonged to John Hancock. The New State House was completed in 1798.

Bulfinch was also the architect for the 1806 expansion of Faneuil Hall. During that project, he doubled its height and width, added a third floor and moved the cupola.

Bulfinch-Designed Otis Mansion on Beacon Hill

Of the four Boston churches he designed, only St. Stephen's on Hanover Street in the North End remains. It was completed in 1804 as the New North Congregational Church. It became Unitarian in 1813, and was sold to the Roman Catholic Diocese of Boston in 1862.

In addition to his public work, Bulfinch influenced the architecture of many private homes in the surrounding Beacon Hill area. Unfortunately, only a few of his private residences survive. Notable are the three mansions he designed for Harrison Grey Otis. The first is at 141 Cambridge Street, the second at 85 Mt. Vernon Street, and the third at 45 Beacon Street.

In addition, there were several other influential architects working in Boston at this time. Another designer in the Federalist style was Asher Benjamin. He designed the Charles Street Meeting House, located on lower Mount Vernon Street at Charles Street. Built between 1804 and 1807, it was originally the Third Baptist Church, which used the Charles River for its baptisms. Also built in this time period was Peter Banner's Sir Christopher Wren inspired Park Street Church – Stop 3.

The North End

To web-translate this chapter:
http://www.stevestravelguide.com/?p=847

Most people know the North End as Boston's Little Italy. But, Italians did not start moving into the North End in any significant number until the 1880's – some 260 years after the North End's earliest residents. The Italians were only the last of a series of ethnic groups to inhabit this area of Boston.

Originally, the North End was a suburb for the Puritan families who migrated to Boston during the 1630's. At that time, it was isolated, virtually an island surrounded by water on three sides and connected to the rest of Boston by a small neck of land.

Old North Church seen looking down Paul Revere Mall

Over time, the land connecting the North End to Boston was filled-in, but the North End remained geographically isolated until the completion of the Big Dig in 2007. In recent history, and prior to the Big Dig's completion, easy entry to the North End was blocked by the elevated Central Artery (Route 93).

By the mid 1640's the North End had evolved into its own distinct community. By 1649, it was large enough to have its own church, the North Meeting House (Boston's Second Church).

In 1659, the North End established its own Burying Ground, Copp's Hill. Copp's Hill took its name from William Copp, a shoemaker who had owned once owned the land. Copp's Hill was also home to a free black population, many of whom are interred in the Burying Ground.

The area around the North Meeting House developed into North Square, which quickly became the center of North End life. At that time, North Square was only one block from the harbor.

Increase Mather, the minister of the North Meeting House, had his home in North Square. It, together with the Meeting House and a number of surrounding buildings, was destroyed in the fire of 1673. The Meeting House was rebuilt, later to be torn down by the British and used for firewood during the Siege of Boston between 1775 and 1776.

North Square today (Revere House is just left of the photo)

The Paul Revere house was constructed in 1680 where Mather's home had once stood. Revere purchased it in 1770 and lived here until the 1780's, when he moved a few blocks away to a house with a harbor view. The Pierce / Hitchborn house, next door to the Revere House, was built around 1711. These houses, along with the Old Corner Book Store and Old State House are the oldest remaining structures in Boston.

The opulent Clark-Frankland and Hutchinson mansions were built after 1710 just off of North Square. Hutchinson's mansion was gutted in 1765 in protest over the Stamp Act. Both the Clark-Frankland and Hutchinson mansions were torn down in 1834 to allow for street widening.

In 1890, Rose Fitzgerald (Kennedy) was born at 4 Garden Court Street, just across the street from where the Hutchinson mansion had stood. Rose later married Joseph P. Kennedy and was the mother of President John F. Kennedy, and Senators Robert and Edward Kennedy. There is a plaque marking the site of her birth on Garden Street just off of North Square. In the mid-1800s, North Square was also home to two Bethels and the Mariners' House. Bethels are churches specifically built to minister to the needs of sailors.

In 1721, construction of the Anglican Christ Church (Old North) began, and was completed in 1723. In 1775, the Christ Church belfry was used to hang the "two if by sea" lanterns that warned Patriots of the British march on Lexington and Concord.

St. Stephens - last Bulfinch-designed Church in Boston

The Charles Bulfinch designed New North Congregational Church on Hanover Street was built between 1802 and 1804. The Church was originally Congregationalist, but it became Unitarian in 1813. It was sold to the Roman Catholic Diocese of Boston in 1862 and is now called St. Stephen's. It is the last Bulfinch designed church standing in Boston.

After the American Revolution, the North End began transitioning to a largely working class neighborhood with the influx of labor associated with the shipping industry. Wharfs and warehouses were built to support maritime trade and shipbuilding. And, along with the often drunken and violent sailors came the requisite gamblers, whores and criminals. To proper Bostonians, it became a dangerous slum, a place to be avoided.

From early on there was an Irish population in Boston. Their numbers were small, but grew to about 7,000 by 1830. The Irish population really swelled during the Great Potato Famine, when a reported 13,000+ Irish moved to Boston during 1847 alone. The North End was their primary destination.

By 1850, over half the North End's population of 23,000 was Irish. This peaked at about 15,000 in 1880. With the influx of new ethnic groups, many of the Irish moved to the South End. By 1890, North End's Irish population had dropped to 5,000 and by the turn of the century it was down to 3,000.

In the 1870's, the North End became home to an Eastern European Jewish population. In the early 1900s, Jews made up almost one third of the North End's population, many settling along Salem Street. By the 1920's, most had moved to Boston's West and South End, then on to Dorchester, Brookline, Newton, Chelsea and Revere.

The last ethnic group to settle in the North End was the Italians. Immigration started in the 1860s with a small group from Genoa. This was followed by an influx from other Italian regions including Sicily, Milan, and Naples. Each regional group settled in its own distinct North End enclave.

By 1900, the North End Italian population had reached 14,000. By 1920, this number reached 37,000, with its peak in 1930 of more than 44,000. The North End was now almost completely Italian - and very crowded!

The census puts today's North End population at about 10,000, of which only 40% are of Italian descent. The remaining residents are a mix of young professionals, college students and others. North End politics are still dominated by Italian Americans.

Feast of St. Anthony, the largest feast in the North End, near the original Regina Pizzeria (1926)

The North End remains Boston's Little Italy, retaining a wonderful "Old Word" feel and a fantastic collection of new and old restaurants, cafes, bakeries and markets. It is one of the most European feeling neighborhoods in America.

It is also the oldest neighborhood in Boston. The North End has been a neighborhood for over 375 years, is home to some of the most important and historic venues in America as well as some of the most significant Freedom Trail sites.

Historic Restaurants

For those visiting the Freedom Trail and wishing an immersive experience, there are a number of historic restaurants directly on or close to the Freedom Trail. The Google Map mentioned in the Maps and Getting Around chapter displays these and other recommended restaurants along with the Freedom Trail Stops.

To auto translate and for a blog posting that includes photos of these restaurants, go to:

http://www.stevestravelguide.com/?p=782

None of these are "fine dining," with the possible exception of The Chart House. All are fun, however, and serve good food. They will absolutely enhance your Freedom Trail experience. Most have excellent lunch specials, including lobster. Enjoy!

Green Dragon Tavern - 1654

11 Marshall Street - on the walk between Faneuil Hall (Stop 11) and the Paul Revere House (Stop 12) in the North End.

The original Green Dragon Tavern was around the corner at 84 Union Street. It was founded in 1654 and became an active pub by 1714. The Green Dragon was a regular haunt for the Sons of Liberty and the site of the Boston Tea Party planning meetings. It was torn down in 1828.

The current Green Dragon incarnation is fun and has decent bar food. It is located on Marshall Street, one of the oldest most authentically historic streets in Boston. Next door is the Ebenezer Hancock House, built in 1767 by John Hancock's uncle, inherited by John and then given to his brother, Ebenezer. Ebenezer became the deputy paymaster to the Continental Army.

Good lunch specials, including lobster. Everyone needs at least one lobster when visiting Boston!

Green Dragon Tavern website:

http://www.somerspubs.com/green-dragon.html

617-367-0055

Union Oyster House - 1742 (1713)

41 Union Street - on the walk between Faneuil Hall (Stop 11) and the Paul Revere House (Stop 12) in the North End.

The Union Oyster House started serving in 1826. It is the oldest continuously operating restaurant in the US. The building, which dates

from 1742 (although other references place it as early as 1713), started its life as a dress shop. At that time, the harbor actually came up to the dress shop's back door. Since then, all of the land that you see has been filled in.

The legendary Oyster Bar at the front of the restaurant is beautiful and historic. Regular customer Daniel Webster sat daily at this bar and drank a tall tumbler of brandy and water with each half-dozen oysters - usually eating at least six plates.

Union Oyster House website:
http://www.unionoysterhouse.com/
617-227-2750

Chart House - John Hancock's Counting House - 1760

60 Long Wharf - 5+ minute walk from the Old State House (Stop 9)

The Chart House was originally the Gardiner House, built on Long Wharf around 1760. Later, it was John Hancock's counting house. It is the oldest building still in use on Long Wharf.

In pleasant weather, it has outside seating with a great view of the harbor and downtown Boston. It is the most elegant restaurant in this collection.

The restaurant offers a 10% AARP discount on food and non-alcoholic beverages.

Chart House website:
http://www.chart-house.com/locations/boston/
617-227-1576

Warren Tavern - 1780

2 Pleasant Street, Charlestown - a short detour on the walk between the USS Constitution (Stop 16) and Bunker Hill (Stop 17)

Built in 1780, the Warren Tavern was reportedly the first building raised after the British burned Charlestown during the Battle of Bunker Hill in 1775. It is named for Doctor and General Joseph Warren, the famous Patriot who was killed at Bunker Hill. It was visited by George Washington, Paul Revere, and Benjamin Franklin.

Good pub food and great slice of history.

Warren Tavern website:
http://warrentavern.com/
617-241-8142

Durgin Park - 1827

340 Faneuil Hall Marketplace - close to Faneuil Hall (Stop 11)

This iconic restaurant, housed in an old warehouse, has been around since 1827, although a restaurant has operated at this spot since 1742. Famous for its old Yankee recipes, it is a real flash from the past and is one of the oldest places you can dine in Boston. Upstairs diners are seated communally at long tables. When the weather is nice, there is outside seating overlooking Quincy Market.

It is a lot of fun and one of the few places you can get Indian Pudding. The roast beef overflows the plate. One of my favorites!

Durgin Park website:

http://www.arkrestaurants.com/durgin_park.html

617-227-2038

Café Marliave - 1875

10 Bosworth Street - close to Boston Latin, Old City Call (Stop 6), but also near Stops 1, 3-8)

The oldest Italian restaurant in Boston, the Marliave dates from 1875. It has lovely outside seating during the summer months.

It located right above of the Province House Steps (1679–1864). The Province House was the official Royal Governor's residence during the Revolutionary period.

Café Marliave website:

http://marliave.com/

617-422-0004

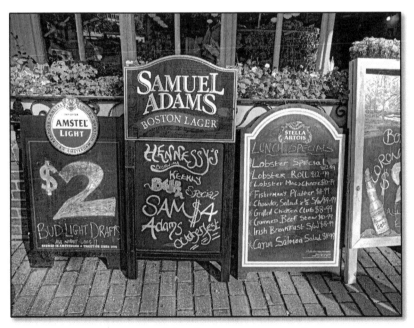

Bargain Lunch by the Green Dragon Tavern

Budget Tips

For a web-based article with auto-translate and web-links to everything mentioned in this chapter, go to:

http://www.stevestravelguide.com/?p=1065

Boston is a big city with big city prices. the Freedom Trail, however, is a tremendous bargain.

Your purchase of this Guide will help you save money during your visit. I've provided the touring information, background context, and access to all other information that you will need to ensure that your visit is a smashing success.

The Google Map and app mentioned in the Introduction chapter is a great companion when visiting or planning you're the Freedom Trail visit. It includes touring information, transportation, directions and even photos of all the Stops and restaurants mentioned in the Guide.

Here are some additional strategies:

Start by visiting one of the two National Park Service Visitor Centers. The NPS personnel are enthusiastic and knowledgeable and are more than willing to help you plan your visit. What they provide is completely free (paid for by US taxpayers), although you may wish to make a small donation. Their tours are very well done - as good as or better than the fee only tours. The new Visitor Center at the base of Faneuil Hall is a real showplace.

The National Park Service has produced a free app that can be downloaded to an Android or iPhone/iPad device. Search Google Play or iTunes for "NPS Boston" to download the app. Keep in mind that it only covers the official 16 Freedom Trail Stops and there is a lot more to see. Use these apps in conjunction with this Guide and the Google Map or app for a complete guide to everything.

Most of the Freedom Trail Stops are free, with the exceptions of the Old South Meeting House, the Old State House, and the Paul Revere House. For those Stops, you can purchase a "Freedom Trail Ticket" available at any of these Stops. It will save you a little more than 20% from purchasing individual adult tickets, and tickets may be used over multiple days. Alternatively, you can purchase it online here, but there is no advantage to purchasing before you arrive.

Another option for visitors is to purchase a bundled package from the Go Select. This package permits entrance to the three admission-charging Stops along with other Boston-area attractions - including a guided tour from TheFreedomTrail.org (a recommended company), museums or a trolley or duck-boat tour. By bundling several attractions together, you can save +/- 20% over individual admissions.

The same company also offers a Go Boston Card. The Go Boston Card is a multiple day ticket to a wide variety of venues. The Cards are expensive, however, and are recommended only if you want to see a number of the supported attractions.

Dining in Boston can be expensive, but bargains are available. Wonderful lunch deals are offered, including lobster, in the Blackstone Block area on the walk between Faneuil Hall (Stop 11) and the Paul Revere House in the North End (Stop 12). Several of the pubs mentioned in the Historic Restaurant section also have reasonably priced good food in a colorful atmosphere.

There are many other good options in and around the North End. Several of my favorites are:

Galleria Umberto, for pizza-oriented lunch fare, is very popular with the locals. 289 Hanover Street (617) 227-5709.

La Summa, old world (not trendy) Italian. Excellent for lunch or dinner. 30 Fleet St 617-523-9503. Check Restaurant.com for coupons.

Pizzeria Regina, Boston's oldest pizzeria, and one of the oldest in the US, established in 1926. The chain started here and this one is much better than the branches. Be prepared to wait for dinner. 11 1/2 Thacher Street. 617-227-0765.

Mike's Pastry on Hanover Street – Cannoli Heaven

There are two well-known and excellent Italian pastry shops on Hanover Street in the North End. On a nice day, pick up a cannoli and wander over to the Paul Revere Mall to sit and enjoy it. **Mike's Pastry,** at 300 Hanover Street, is larger and has inside seating. **Modern Pastry** is across the street from Mike's, at 257 Hanover Street. You can't go wrong with either one.

Inside the Faneuil Hall Marketplace "Quincy Market Colonnade" there is a large food court. This is similar to what you will find in many shopping malls, but there are many Boston-area restaurants represented.

Other good inexpensive restaurant options can be researched via Boston.com's Cheap Eats web listings.

Public transportation is the best way to get around the city, and if your trip spans several days, a multi-day pass may be in order. Children 11 and under are free, and junior-high and high school students are eligible for a 50% discount. You'll need an ID and specials ticket that may not be available at all locations.

There is a fun and scenic ten minute **Water Shuttle** ride across the inner harbor between Long Wharf (by the Chart House restaurant and the Aquarium - near Faneuil Hall and the Old State House) and the Charlestown Navy Yard (near the USS Constitution). It is part of the MBTA system - the single ride fare is only $3 for adults, with children (2 per adult) free. It is called the F4 route.

Definitely pick up a free **CharlieCard.** The CharlieCard is a reusable and re-loadable plastic ticket for use on the MBTA. You can get a CharlieCard at transit stations and many MBTA ticket counters by asking a Service Agent. By showing the card, you receive discounts on attractions such as FreedomTrail.org tours, Boston Duck Tours (a fun way to spend an afternoon), restaurant discounts, and more. To learn what discounts are available, search for and download the "CharlieCard discount booklet".

CityPASS for Boston is similar to the Go Boston Card mentioned above, but as of now, it only offers entrance to five attractions (the New England Aquarium, the Museum of Science, Skywalk Observatory, the Museum of Fine Arts, and one entrance to the Harvard Museum of Natural History or Revolutionary Boston at the Old State House). If you plan to visit several of these, it may be worthwhile.

Restaurant.com is a good source for restaurant coupons, but be sure to read the fine print. Search for "Restaurant.com coupon codes" as they often run discounts from their normal rates.

Parking is expensive, but there are a few bargains to be had around the Charlestown Navy Yard. Park there and walk or take the Water Shuttle to the downtown sites. The Nautica Garage at 88 Constitution Road, directly across from the Navy Yard's entrance, has discounted rates if you get your ticket validated at the National Park Service Visitor Center.

Closer to the downtown sites, there are a few all day parking specials near the Aquarium on Atlantic Avenue, but most require that you enter early (before 8:30 AM) and leave after 4 PM. Some competitive rates can be found on Commercial Street in the North End. If you are driving, an internet search to identify your options is encouraged. The **Parkopedia.com** website is a good place to start your search.

Galleria Umberto in the North End

Fruit in the Haymarket Open-Air Market

Sources

Primary:

The following books were used as primary sources:

Boston: A Topographical History, Lawrence W. Kennedy, Walter Muir Whitehill. Belknap Press; Third Edition, Enlarged edition (2000).

Bunker Hill, A City, A Siege, A Revolution, Nathaniel Philbrick. Viking, New York; (2013).

Freedom by the Bay: The Boston Freedom Trail, William G. Schofield. Branden Pub Co; 2nd edition (1988).

New England Frontier Puritans and Indians 1620-1675, Alden T. Vaughan. Little Brown and Company; Boston, (1965).

Paul Revere's Ride, David Hackett Fischer. Oxford University Press (April 19, 1995).

Planning the City upon a Hill: Boston Since 1630, Lawrence W. Kennedy. University of Massachusetts Press (1994).

Puritan Experiment New England Society from Bradford to Edwards, Francis J. Bremer University Press of New England (1995).

Redcoats and Rebels, Christopher Hibbert. Pen and Sword (June 2008).

The Hub: Boston Past and Present, Thomas H. O'Connor. Northeastern University Press, Boston (2001).

The North End: A Brief History of Boston's Oldest Neighborhood, Alex R. Goldfeld. The History Press (2009).

The Whites of their Eyes: Bunker Hill, the First American Army, and the Emergence of George Washington, Paul Lockhart. Harper (2011).

Secondary:

The following books were also referred to in the development of the Guide. Many of these are old books available for free download from Google Books and other public domain sources.

A Topographical and Historical Description of Boston, Nathaniel B. Shurtleff. Boston, Printed by Request of the City Council (1871).

The Book of Boston, Fifty Years' Recollections of the New England Metropolis, Edwin M. Bacon, editor. The Book of Boston Company (1916)

The History of New England from 1630 to 1639, original manuscript with notes, John Winthrop, Esq. Phelps and Farnham (1825).

The making of New England, 1580 - 1643, Samuel Adams Drake. Charles Scribner's Sons (1886).

Bowens Picture of Boston, Third Edition. Otis, Broaders and Company (1838)

The True Story of Paul Revere, His Midnight Ride, His Arrest and Court Marshall, His Useful Public Services, Charles Ferris Gettemy. Little Brown and Company (1905)

The Frigate Constitution, The Central Figure of the Navy Under Sail, Ira N. Hollis. Houghton, Mifflin and Company (1900)

Faneuil Hall & Faneuil Hall Market, Adam English Brown. Lee and Shepard (1900).

A History of Boston, Caleb Hopkins Snow. Bowen (1825)

Battle of Bunker Hill, Richard Frothingham. Little Brown and Company (1890)

History of Siege of Boston and the Battles of Lexington, Concord, and Bunker Hill, Richard Frothingham. Little Brown and Company (1896)

Mapping Boston, edited by Alex Krieger and David Cobb. The Muriel G. and Norman B. Leventhal Family Foundation (1999)

Illustrations and Photographs:

All photographs are by the author and Copyright © 2012 Steve Gladstone, all rights reserved

All historic or other illustrations from external sources are licensed under the Creative Commons Attribution 2.0 Generic or Share Alike 2.5 Generic or other similar licenses as specified in their source (listed below).

The historic images (or other media files) are in the public domain because their copyright has expired. This applies to U.S. works where the copyright has expired, often because its first publication occurred prior to January 1, 1923 or the life of the author plus 100 years. Please see the source for additional information and associated PD-Art tag.

Other works are in the public domain in the United States because they are works prepared by an officer or employee of the United States Government as part of that person's official duties under the terms of Title 17, Chapter 1, Section 105 of the US Code.

Sources of the files and other information are noted below. Please note that most of these files have been enhanced and/or annotated for this book. For original documents and additional license information, please reference the source.

Listed in order of appearance:

Extract from the **Park Map with Outline of 1775 Boston Shoreline** is from the National Park Service. Source: this and other park maps are available from the National Park Service website, http://www.nps.gov/bost/planyourvisit/maps.htm

Cutting down Beacon Hill, c. 1800. Scanned from "Boston: A Guide Book" by Edwin M. Bacon, Ginn and Company, Publishers, 29 Beacon Street, Boston, the Atheneum Press, 1903. Copyright 1903 By Ginn & Company. Source: http://en.wikipedia.org/wiki/File:1800_beacon_hill.jpg

Quincy Market and Faneuil Hall in 1838 Source: http://en.wikipedia.org/wiki/File:QuincyHall_Bowen_PictureOfBoston_1838.jpg

Extract from Map of Boston in Before 1645. Based on Bonner's map of 1722, by Annie Thwing, 1914. Source: http://www.doak.ws/boston1643Map.jpg

Plan of Boston proper, showing changes in street and wharf lines, 1795 to 1895, (annotated), Perkins, Charles Carroll. From the Norman B. Leventhal Map Center at the Boston Public Library. Source: http://maps.bpl.org/id/124711768

Revere Engraving of British Troops Landing in Boston Source: http://en.wikipedia.org/wiki/File:Boston_1768.jpg

Revere Engraving of Boston Massacre Source: http://en.wikipedia.org/wiki/File:Boston_Massacre_high-res.jpg

Boston Tea Party lithograph by Sarony & Major from National Archives ID 532892. Source http://commons.wikimedia.org/wiki/File:Boston_tea_party.jpg

National Park Service Map of the British Expedition and the Patriot Messengers on April 18-19 (Paul Revere's Ride and the Battles of Lexington and Concord) Source: http://en.wikipedia.org/wiki/File:Concord_Expedition_and_Patriot_Messengers.jpg

US Military Academy Map of First Assault on Bunker Hill Source: http://en.wikipedia.org/wiki/File:Bunker_hill_first_attack.gif Maps of the second and third attacks are at http://en.wikipedia.org/wiki/File:Bunker_hill_second_attack.gif and http://en.wikipedia.org/wiki/File:Bunker_hill_final_attack.gif

Map extract from **"A plan of the town of Boston with the entrenchments &ca. of His Majesty's forces in 1775"**, from the observations of Lieut. Page of His Majesty's Corps of Engineers, and from those of other gentlemen." From the US Library of Congress. Source - http://www.loc.gov/item/gm71000624/

Additional Important Links & References

Note: This is a listing of important reference and useful websites, some have been used in the creation of this book. Other specific Stop or event sites are embedded throughout the Guide.
American Antiquarian Society website: http://americanantiquarian.org/
Boston 1775 Blogspot website: . http://boston1775.blogspot.com/
Boston By Foot website: http://www.bostonbyfoot.org/about/
Boston Tea Party Historical Society website: http://www.boston-tea-party.org
Boston Public Transportation website. http://www.mbta.com/
Concord Magazine Concord Fight : http://www.concordma.com/concordfight/toc.html
The Freedom Trail Foundation website: http://www.thefreedomtrail.org/

Google map of The Freedom Trail of official and unofficial Stops mentioned in this Guide website: http://goo.gl/maps/LhFl.

iBoston History and Architecture website: http://www.iboston.org/index2.php

Bostonian Society **Mapping Revolutionary Boston** website: http://www.bostonhistory.org/sub/mappingrevolutionaryboston/

Massachusetts Bay Transportation Authority (MBTA) website (QR below): http://mbta.com/

Mass Historical Society The Coming of the American Revolution website: http://www.masshist.org/revolution/

National Heritage Museum Sowing the Seeds of Liberty website: http://www.nationalheritagemuseum.org/Exhibitions/CurrentExhibitions/SowingtheSeedsofLiberty LexingtonandtheAme.aspx

National Park Visitor Centers website (QR below): http://www.nps.gov/bost/planyourvisit/visitorcenters.htm

National Park Map with Outline of 1775 Boston Shoreline pdf: http://www.nps.gov/bost/planyourvisit/upload/BOSTpark%20overlay.pdf

National Park Service Boston website: http://www.nps.gov/bost/planyourvisit/index.htm

National Park Service Minuteman Park website (QR below): http://www.nps.gov/mima/index.htm

StevesTravelGuide (the author's) website: http://www.stevestravelguide.com.

Worcester Polytechnic Institute **Battle of Lexington and Concord** website: http://www.wpi.edu/academics/military/lexcon.html

Norman B. Leventhal Map Center at the Boston Library website: http://maps.bpl.org/explore/location/boston-mass-7

YouTube Channel of containing supplementary material including Stops & Sites mentioned in the Guide website: http://www.youtube.com/user/stevestravelguide

Important Traveler QR Codes (all mentioned in prior section):

Natl Park Svc Boston   StevesTravelGuide   MBTA   Google Map of Trail

Index

The Freedom Trail winding through the North End around the corner from the Paul Revere House & North Square

Signs on Hanover Street in the North End - Boston's Little Italy

Marshall Street in the Blackstone Block by the Green Dragon Tavern - one of the oldest streets in Boston (c.1652)

USS Constitution in the Charlestown Navy Yard

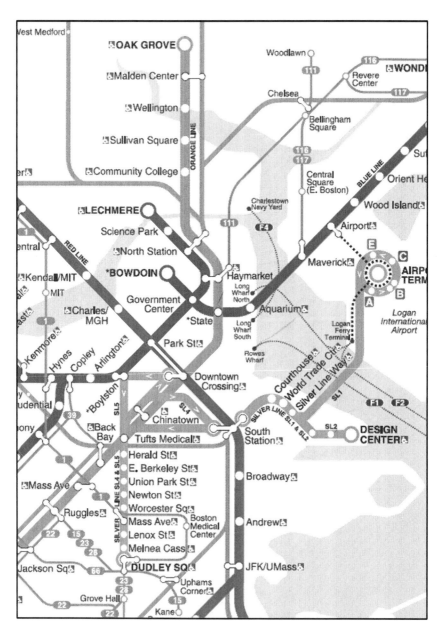

Downtown MBTA Stops